enchanted circles:
flower garlands, swags and wreaths

enchanted circles:
flower garlands, swags and wreaths

over 200 projects for beautiful
fresh and dried arrangements

fiona barnett & terence moore

southwater

This edition is published by Southwater

Southwater is an imprint of Anness Publishing Ltd
Hermes House, 88–89 Blackfriars Road, London SE1 8HA
tel. 020 7401 2077; fax 020 7633 9499
www.southwaterbooks.com; info@anness.com

© Anness Publishing Ltd 1999, 2003

This edition distributed in the UK by The Manning Partnership Ltd,
6 The Old Dairy, Melcombe Road, Bath BA2 3LR;
tel. 01225 478 444; fax 01225 478 440; sales@manning-partnership.co.uk

This edition distributed in the USA and Canada by National Book Network,
4720 Boston Way, Lanham, MD 20706; tel. 301 459 3366; fax 301 459 1705; www.nbnbooks.com

This edition distributed in Australia by Pan Macmillan Australia,
Level 18, St Martins Tower, 31 Market St, Sydney, NSW 2000;
tel. 1300 135 113; fax 1300 135 103; customer.service@macmillan.com.au

This edition distributed in New Zealand by The Five Mile Press (NZ) Ltd,
PO Box 33–1071 Takapuna, Unit 11/101–111 Diana Drive, Glenfield, Auckland 10;
tel. (09) 444 4144; fax (09) 444 4518; fivemilenz@clear.net.nz

A CIP catalogue record for this book is available from the British Library.

Publisher: Joanna Lorenz
Project Editor: Felicity Forster
Text: Fiona Barnett, Stephanie Donaldson, Roger Egerickx,
Kathy Ellis, Tessa Evelegh, Beverley Jollands,
Gilly Love, Terence Moore, Ercole Moroni,
Pamela Westland, Editor: Judy Cox
Designers: Nigel Partridge, Ian Sandom
Stylists: Tessa Evelegh, Michelle Garrett,
Gilly Love, Leeann Mackenzie
Photographers: Andrew Cameron, James Duncan, Michelle Garrett,
Nelson Hargreaves, Debbie Patterson, Polly Wreford
Index: Dawn Butcher
Editorial Reader: Marion Wilson
Production Controller: Ann Childers

Previously published as *Garlands, Circles and Decoratives Wreaths*

1 3 5 7 9 10 8 6 4 2

CONTENTS
· · ·

INTRODUCTION 6
FRESH MATERIALS 10
CARE OF CUT FLOWERS 12
DRIED MATERIALS 14
EQUIPMENT 18
TECHNIQUES 20

WREATHS AND GARLANDS   26

SWAGS AND HANGINGS   84

RINGS AND CIRCLETS   122

HEARTS, STARS AND
OTHER SHAPED WREATHS   170

SPECIAL OCCASIONS   202

SUPPLIERS AND INDEX 252

INTRODUCTION

• • •

*Before beginning a project, you need to
think about what materials to use. This
section gives a guide to some of the most
commonly used fresh and dried materials,
as well as information about how to care for
cut flowers, the equipment you will need,
and step-by-step techniques for making perfect
garlands, circles and wreaths every time.*

Right: Save the best roses of the season and use them to make pretty, fresh wreaths.

Below: For a really special dessert, decorate glass bowls with rings of flowers and leaves.

Garlands, circles and decorative wreaths take floral decorations beyond vases and bowls, and give you the scope to make wonderful, large-scale statements when you are decorating your home for a special occasion. They will enhance architectural features of which you are particularly fond, and give a feeling of opulence and generosity in keeping with a festive mood. Don't save these decorations only for grand occasions, however. Simply decorated twig or wicker rings make charming wall ornaments almost anywhere, while a rope of herbs is beautiful and useful in the kitchen.

Before you begin, think carefully about the scale of your decoration. For example, check that your Christmas wreath will be in proportion to your front door, and cut ropes for swags and hangings generously enough to enable them to drape beautifully. If you are making a long swag, you may find it easier to construct it in several shorter sections which can be joined afterwards. Dried material in particular can be quite stiff, and trying to bend a garland into shape after it is finished may create gaps that are difficult to hide.

The amount of material you will need for your garlands, circles and wreaths will depend on the size of your finished decoration. For a lavish effect, base your design on something that you can get plenty of, such as evergreens from your own garden.

BEING CREATIVE

Over the past few years, an enormous range of high-quality floral material has become widely available in florists' shops. It is now possible to buy exotic dried fruits from the Far East alongside traditional home-grown flowers such as roses, solidago and lavender.

If you are making a dried wreath or garland, you can keep the costs down by drying some of the materials yourself. The simplest method is to air-dry flowers and foliage by hanging them upside-down in bunches, loosely wrapped in open-ended paper, in a warm, dry place. This technique works for most plants but some, such as ferns, become very brittle.

Below: A display made from a single material looks very effective. This wreath is made from fresh eucalyptus foliage.

As well as the bewildering choice of home-produced and exotic materials available from florists, you can also collect a great deal of useful material yourself on a woodland walk or on a beach. Autumn especially is a good time to find woodland treasures in lovely rich gold and earthy-brown colours. Fungi, twigs, fir cones, driftwood, seashells and seed pods have interesting shapes and textures which you can use in many displays, with or without flowers. Red chillies, now readily available in supermarkets, add a vivid splash of colour to a Christmas display and can even be used on their own for a bold, modern look.

DESIGNING

You often require more material than you think for a display, so it is a good idea to start with a small project first. As you begin to learn some techniques and gain confidence with them, you can tackle some more ambitious displays using more expensive materials. Plenty of space is needed in which to work when you are making large projects, so that you can lay out your materials around you.

Feel free to adapt the materials listed for each project and don't be afraid to experiment; you will soon find the confidence to create your own individual displays which exactly suit the position they are intended for.

A major innovation in wreath-making in recent years is the glue gun. This is a vital piece of equipment, enabling you to assemble materials quickly and easily. Several of the dried flower designs are created entirely by this method, while others employ a mixture of techniques.

DEVELOPING SKILLS

Take the time to master the basic skills described in the Techniques section, and refer back to them when they are mentioned in a project. Give yourself time to read the instructions for the project thoroughly. As you work, clear away all the cut-off stems and other waste material so that you can stand back frequently and look at your design in progress. View it from different angles, thinking about the visual relationships of colour, shape, height and texture. It is very easy to keep adding material while losing sight of the overall plan.

Aim to build up a display so that delicate flowers such as roses and peonies are added last, reducing the risk of damaging the flowerheads. Try, if possible, to complete a display in one day; it is often hard to go back to it without changing course slightly. Once you have finished a display, it is best not to rework it any more than you have to in case you spoil its initial freshness and vitality. Knowing when to leave a display alone is a skill that comes with practice.

If you are new to arranging, there are plenty of simple, straightforward projects to start with that will help you acquire a good range of skills before moving on to more ambitious displays. Once you have gained confidence with your tools and the basic techniques, you will be able to design and create your own personal works of art from the wonderful variety of materials ready to inspire you. All you really need to create a display that you can be proud of is the courage to plunge in and make a start.

Whether you are planning a grand occasion or are just feeling creative, you'll find plenty of inspiration in this collection of enchanting, natural decorations.

Above: Golden candle rings decorated with sticks of cinnamon make lovely aromatic Christmas centrepieces.

Top left: Ring designs can be as large or as small as you like. If you can find lots of fresh mistletoe, combine it with ribbons and berries to make a traditional kissing ring.

Below: For a special outdoor celebration, adorn a table with a swag of wild-looking flowers.

FRESH MATERIALS
· · ·

A garland of freshly picked flowers makes a beautiful and highly individual gift, and is also a pleasure to make. You need to locate your chosen flowers, plan your harvesting time with precision, care for the freshly picked blooms, and learn how to assemble them in a pleasing design that balances colour and form.

It doesn't matter if you don't have access to fields of wild flowers or your own garden plot – one of the most important factors in allowing the flower arranger more creative freedom has been the enormous improvement in the availability and good quality of commercially grown cut flowers. The flower arranger is no longer restricted by the seasonal availability of the majority of popular cut blooms and has an ever-growing range of flowers to work with. Further, modern growing techniques have improved the quality and increased the life span of cut flowers; for example, the few days' cut life of sweet peas has been extended to a week or more.

All of these improvements give today's fresh flower arranger more options in terms of choice of materials, colour palette and arranging techniques.

HARVESTING AND SELECTING FRESH MATERIALS
No matter how casual or carefully calculated an arrangement may be, one consideration is paramount: all the plant material in the display must be in perfect condition. This means you must harvest materials from the garden or countryside when they are in the peak of condition, and be critically selective whenever you purchase flowers from a florist's or market stall.

In general, it is best to leave flowers to reach a mid-way stage of maturity on the plant. It is important to plan your harvesting time with something of the precision of a farmer garnering his crops. Avoid cutting flowers and foliage in the heat of the sun, and when they are at their most vulnerable and least able to recover from the transition from growing plant to design component. In any case, especially in hot weather, it is best to put stems straight into water as soon as they are cut. For large quantities of stems, this may mean taking a bucket of cool water from patch to patch.

CHAMOMILE
(Chamaemelum nobile)
Reminiscent of a summer meadow, chamomile has daisy-like flowers, the stems of which can be pushed into a foam ring. The foam needs to be kept well-watered to prolong the life of the display.

DAFFODILS
Bright spring daffodils can be used in a foam ring to make a striking Easter wreath. Handle the stems carefully, cutting them to a length of about 7.5 cm (3 in).

DAISIES
Take care when making a garland from daisies as their stems are very supple and delicate. You should make daisy rings at the last minute and water them well to keep them fresh.

White daisies are fresh and simple, and look charming as napkin rings.

EUCALYPTUS
Fresh eucalyptus is ideal for making wreaths because it is very strong, but not rigid. In addition, its bluey-green shades are most sympathetic to many colour schemes. There are many varieties, each with different shaped leaves. Once hung up, a fresh eucalyptus wreath will dry naturally.

Eucalyptus is robust but not rigid, so is ideal for using in a fresh wreath.

HELLEBORUS NIGER
(Hellebores)
Hellebore flowers have delicate nodding heads and can range in colour from white to green, and palest pink to softest burgundy. They are a long-lasting winter flower, making their appearance late in winter and continuing to flower right through to spring. If you can't find these, you could substitute white anemones for a similar effect.

HYDRANGEAS
There is an enormous range of hydrangea colours, from white through pinks, greens, blues and reds to deep purples, making them an excellent choice for fresh garlands.

Subtle, pastel-coloured hydrangeas look good in tightly packed arrangements.

IVY
Ivy trails provide useful foliage for fresh swag displays as they can be entwined with other materials.

LAVENDER
(Lavandula)
Lavender is an extraordinarily versatile and resilient plant, growing well in the sun-drenched countries of the Mediterranean and the damp northern climes of the Pacific Northwest and the Midwest. When buying lavender, try to get a bunch that has densely packed florets, and make sure you buy enough for your design – one bunch or even a specific number of stems can be misleading, so the best solution is to buy as much lavender as you can afford, then work out how much area it would cover by measuring the space taken up by the tips of the flower spikes.

Fresh lavender is one of nature's delights, with a fragrance as beguiling as its colour.

LILAC
Lilac flowers are at their best in late spring. Once cut, their stems can be pushed into a foam ring to make a simple fresh circle for a table decoration.

MARJORAM
Marjoram is a good herb to add to foam rings and, like many herbs, can be taken out afterwards and hung up to dry for future use in a dried garland or wreath.

PARROT TULIPS
These flowers have spectacular red and yellow spreading petals, and can be used to great effect in foam rings – especially in candle rings because they look like flames licking up the side of the candle. Parrot tulips can have their lives extended by shortening their stems.

PARSLEY
Fresh parsley makes a pretty, leafy addition to a garland or wreath. Once made up, you might need to spray the display so that the leaves receive some moisture. After a couple of days you may wish to dismantle the garland and dry the herbs for use in another project.

MENTHA X PIPERITA
(Peppermint)
Mint is inclined to wilt easily when used in a foam ring, so water well and make up your circlet at the last minute. Once finished, you will need to spray the ring with water from time to time.

ROSMARINUS
(Rosemary)
As well as being attractive to look at, the distinctive aroma of fresh rosemary adds to the ambience of garlands and wreaths. Rosemary lasts well out of water – the woodiness of the stems means that they retain their freshness for longer – so they are ideal for using in decorative displays.

ROSA
(Roses)
Roses are always a favourite choice, and can be enjoyed all year round. Garden roses start blooming in mid-spring and continue into late autumn if the weather is mild. During the barren winter months there are still hundreds of commercially grown roses to choose from. Try to buy buds a few days before they are needed to ensure that they open in time to make a stunning display.

Garden and wild roses look pretty combined with cow parsley.

SALVIA
(Sage)
The soft grey-green tones and generous proportions of sage make it a highly effective herb for floral decorations. It is also deliciously aromatic when used fresh in garlands.

SPRUCE
Spruce, or blue pine, can be used in a long-lasting fresh wreath and then left to dry out later. It has a lovely aromatic scent and makes a magnificent Christmas decoration.

CARE OF CUT FLOWERS
· · ·

CONDITIONING

Conditioning is the term for the process of preparing flowers and foliage for use in arranging.

The general rules are: remove all lower leaves to ensure there is no soft material below the water level where it will rot, form bacteria and shorten the life of the arrangement; cut the stem ends at an angle to provide as large a surface area as possible for the

take-up of water; and, finally, stand all materials in cold water for a couple of hours to encourage the maximum intake of water before use.

For many varieties of flower and foliage this treatment is perfectly adequate; for some, however, there are a number of additional methods to increase their longevity.

BOILING WATER

The woody stems of lilac, guelder rose and rhododendron, the sap-filled stems of milkweed (euphorbia) and poppy, even roses and chrysan-themums, will benefit from the shock treatment of immersing their stem ends in boiling water.

Remove all lower foliage, together with approximately 6 cm (2½ in) of bark from the ends of woody stems. Cut the stem ends at an angle of 45 degrees and, in the case of woody stems, split up to approximately 6 cm (2½ in) from the bottom. Wrap any flowerheads in paper to protect them from the hot steam.

Carefully pour boiling water into a heatproof container to a depth of

approximately 6 cm (2½ in) and plunge the bottoms of the stems into the hot water, leaving them for two to three minutes before removing and plunging them into deep cold water. The heat of the boiling water will have dispelled air from the stems to enable the efficient take-up of cold water. The boiling water will also have destroyed bacteria on the stem ends.

Wilted roses can also be revived by having their stems recut and given the boiling water treatment, and then left standing (with their heads wrapped up to their necks) in cold water for two hours.

The rose stripper (below) is invaluable when dealing with very thorny stems.

SEARING

Searing is a method of extending the lives of plants such as milkweed (euphorbia) and poppies which contain a milky sap, the release of which affects the water quality.

It involves passing the stem end through a flame until it is blackened, then placing it in tepid water. This forms a layer of charcoal to seal the stem end, preventing sap leakage but still allowing the take-up of water.

HOLLOW STEMS

Delphiniums, amaryllis and lupins have hollow stems and the best method of conditioning them is to turn them upside-down and literally fill them with water.

To keep the water in the stem, form a plug from cotton wool or tissue and carefully bung the open stem end. Tie a rubber band around the base of the stem to avoid splitting, then stand the stem in tepid water. The water trapped inside the stem will keep it firm and the cotton wool will help draw more water up into it.

FOLIAGE

Generally the rules for conditioning foliage are the same as for flowers. It is vital to strip the lower leaves and cut the stem base at an angle. Depending on the stem structure and size, other special techniques may well apply. It is also important to scrape the bark from the bottom 6 cm (2½ in) of the stem

and split it to further encourage the take-up of water and thereby prolong the life of the foliage.

WRAPPING TO STRAIGHTEN STEMS

Some flowers, such as gerbera, have soft, flexible weak stems and other flowers may simply have wilted. There is a technique for strengthening such material: take a group of flowers and wrap the top three-quarters of

their stems together in paper to keep them erect, then stand them in deep cool water for about two hours. The cells within the stems will fill with water and be able to stand on their own when the paper is removed.

ETHYLENE GAS

Ethylene is an odourless gas emitted by such things as rubbish (garbage), exhaust fumes, fungi and ripening fruit. It has the effect of accelerating the rate at which some flowers mature which in turn causes non-opening and dropping of buds and yellowing of leaves. Particularly susceptible are carnations, freesia, alstroemeria and roses. Be aware of this when using fruit in a flower arrangement.

DRIED MATERIALS
. . .

The range of dried flowers and materials is enormous and your local florist will be able to advise you.

BUYING MATERIALS
There are a few general rules to bear in mind when selecting materials. Make sure the stock is bright in colour and not too brittle. Check the flowers for moth damage, especially roses and peonies. Look inside the flowers for grubs or eggs. All dried flowers will lose some material when handled, but avoid any that drop a lot of petals.

If shop-bought flowers have dried out, hang them in a moist room such as the kitchen or bathroom for a day or two to absorb some moisture and make them much easier to work with. Don't leave them longer or they may become too damp and start to rot. If they feel too soft after a couple of days, reverse the process by placing them in a dry, warm airing cupboard.

USING FRESH MATERIALS
Branches, twigs and moss can be used fresh, in fact they are much easier to work with when a little damp. Displays using these items must be left in a warm, dry place to dry out.

DRYING MATERIALS
Air-drying is the easiest and most successful method, in a place with a constant flow of warm, dry air, such as an airing cupboard or a space above a slow-burning oven. Dry woody items on a wire rack; they may take some time. Flowers can be tied and hung upside-down and will take much less time. If the drying space is light, cover or wrap the materials with newspaper, making sure that air can still circulate around them. Experiment – even daffodils can be dried, producing wonderful results.

Ambrosina has a strong and attractive scent that is wonderful to work with.

ACHILLEA FILIPENDULINA
(Golden yarrow)
This mustard-yellow plant has been a favourite for many years. The large heads fill spaces quickly in any large, country-style arrangement. They are easy to keep dust-free.

ACHILLEA PTARMICA
Clusters of small, bright white flowers on dark green stems. Use with care; the bright white tends to stand out when combined with other materials. They have a very long life but need to be kept away from damp or the white will turn to pale brown very quickly.

ALCHEMILLA MOLLIS
(Lady's mantle)
This is a beautiful material to use; it can be added to all types of displays and gives a soft feel. However, in time, the colour will fade to a soft yellow-brown. Take care when using, as it tends to break quite readily. Alchemilla is very easy to grow.

AMARANTHUS
(Love-lies-bleeding)
Most commonly seen either in natural dark green or dyed dark red. May be long and upright, but also available as a long, soft tail. Be selective when choosing bunches; their thickness and length vary tremendously. For small display work, use the thinner variety. *Amaranthus caudatus* is particularly attractive and has a pale green colour.

AMBROSINA
Widely available in two versions, short and long, this is a pale green plant. As with all green material, avoid strong light. In a centrally heated house it will dry out and become very fragile, so keep it away from the heat.

ANAPHALIS MARGARITACEA
(Pearl everlasting)
A fluffy white flower that is extremely easy to grow. The flowers dry in the garden on the stem. Make sure you pick them before they go to seed, or you will have a room full of fluff.

BUPLEURUM GRIFFITHII
This green plant is a useful filler. Care needs to be taken when using it in light conditions, because the green will fade fast. Each stem has a large number of heads with small seeds.

CARTHAMUS
Available with and without flowers; the dark ginger flower is used to make dye. A stunning addition to a display, the bunches tend to be fairly large and need to be split and wired. Choose flowers which have deep green leaves and dark orange flowers.

The greeny-yellow centre of anaphalis makes it match well with other materials.

Larkspur is a popular flower and is available in a range of attractive colours.

CHINESE LANTERN
(Physalis)
The vivid orange colour of the paper-thin lanterns will not last if exposed to strong light. It is a fairly easy plant to grow in the garden.

COPPER BEECH
(Fagus sylvatica)
The dark brown leaf makes a good backdrop. In their natural condition, the leaves tend to curl as they dry.

The globe-shaped heads of Echinops are a deep steely-blue at their best.

ECHINOPS RITRO
(Globe thistle)
Handle with care as the delicate blue heads are prone to break apart. The new season's stock handles much better. Echinops are quite expensive but are also very easy to grow in the right conditions.

ECHINOPS SPHAEROCEPHALUS
The same family but much larger, with spiky silvery-blue heads. They take spray colour very well. Handle with care.

EUCALYPTUS
Available mostly as a preserved (dried) product, this wonderful leaf normally comes in two colours, green and brown. A joy to work with, because it gives off a beautiful scent when the stems and leaves are bruised. Ideal for large displays that require long stems.

EVERLASTING *see* Strawflower

FIR CONES
Look out for fir cones as autumn turns to winter. There are many varieties, from tiny larch cones to larger pine cones. Fir cones look wonderful when gilded with spray paint – this should always be done in a well ventilated area, and allow the cones to dry completely before using.

GLOBE ARTICHOKE
(Cynara cardunculus)
These make a huge statement and deserve to be displayed alone. The outside comes in a range of green and purple; the centre is a mass of delicate mauve fronds. To dry them, hang them upside-down, wrapped in paper with the bottom open over a constant flow of warmth for 2–3 weeks.

GOLDEN MUSHROOMS
These are often found with ready-fixed stems; if yours have no stems add them with a glue gun. A light spray of clear florist's lacquer will bring out the rich colours.

GRASSES *see* Wheat

HOLLY OAK
(Banksia serrata)
This very large leaf is usually preserved (dried). It makes a good substitute for holly and will not lose its shape or dry out.

HYDRANGEA MACROPHYLLA
One of the most useful dried materials, in a range of colours from very dark pink through to a pale almost-grey and a variety of tones to dark blue. Can be dried very easily at home, in a light-free, warm area. The large heads have a very long life.

IMMORTELLE
(Xeranthemum)
Small, star-shaped, mostly purple or white flowers with an extremely long shelf life, these tolerate bright light very well. Often used as a filler because they are inexpensive, but the strong purple colour will dominate a display.

KUTCHI FRUIT
An exotic caramel-coloured seed pod with a vanilla aroma. It combines well with woodland materials.

LARKSPUR
(Consolida)
Very close to the delphinium, these flowers come in a range of colours but are most commonly blue, pink or white. If the bunches are a little crushed, revive them with very gentle steaming. Probably one of the most useful display flowers, it is a pretty flower and ideal for summer displays.

You can spray Holly Oak with paint or gild lightly with gold for a special look.

Not only does lavender look and smell attractive, it is also easy to work with.

LAVENDER
(Lavandula)

Dutch lavender is a pale-coloured lavender, with uniform stems and a strong scent. French lavender (*Lavandula stoechas*) is a magnificent rich blue. Take care when buying, because the quality often varies. Lavender is a popular display filler.

MARIGOLD
(Tagetes erecta)

Bright yellow or orange, this makes a spectacular splash of colour. Choose flowers with as little damage as possible. They look almost fresh and can even be arranged alone around a wreath or garland.

MARJORAM
(Origanum marjorana)

This dark purple and green herb works well with dried materials such as roses, peonies, nigella and lavender.

MINT
(Mentha)

This pale purple flower looks very uninspiring alone, but combined with other materials it makes a good partner. It gives off a lovely scent.

MINTOLA BALLS

These woody seed pods look similar to small coconuts. They are often supplied with wooden stakes.

MOSSES

The main types of moss used in this book are sphagnum, tillandsia, green wood, lichen and reindeer moss. Although all can be purchased dried, only tillandsia moss is really suitable for use in this condition; the other varieties are best used slightly damp then left to dry out in the display. You can also buy different coloured mosses to suit your display.

NICANDRA
(Physalodes)

This green seed pod is a smaller alternative to the orange Chinese lantern. The pale colour can be used with many other colours and the shape gives a distinctive texture to an arrangement. Keep it away from direct sunlight. In time, the green will turn dark brown but for a seed pod this is quite acceptable.

NIGELLA DAMASCENA
(Love-in-a-mist)

A real favourite, these seed pods combine purple and green colours with an unusual shape. However, they dislike bright light and will fade very fast. A good material for special-occasion displays. Enhance or change their colour using spray paints.

NIGELLA ORIENTALIS

The same family as love-in-a-mist, but a completely different shape. All-green, it is susceptible to loss of colour. Usually it has quite a short season, so is not always available.

OAK
(Quercus)

This leaf is used in a similar way to preserved (dried) copper beech. It tends to be a little thicker and will stand the test of time even better. It often has a little brown dye added to give a dark, rich colour.

OREGANO
(Origanum vulgare)

This well-loved herb makes a dried plant that can be used over and over again. It has a very unusual texture and a beautiful scent. The colour will keep indefinitely. Any unused pieces can be kept for a pot-pourri, mixed with lavender and rose petals.

PEONY
(Paeonia)

These have a very short season. Although expensive to buy, they are quite easy to dry at home, if you are careful. Mostly dark pink, they can also be a rich pinky-cream. Moths love peonies so make sure that there are no eggs in the flowers.

POPPY SEED HEAD
(Papaver)

Although these are very common, they range from dark powder-grey through to greeny-grey, and will suit most colour schemes. Avoid spraying them with clear florist's lacquer, which will destroy the powdery bloom. Do not use the seeds on food.

PROTEA COMPACTA
(Cape honey flower)

This woody head will last for ever and needs only a light dusting to maintain its good looks. A range of different sizes is available. Use a strong pair of cutters to cut the stems.

Nicandra have a pale colour and attractive rounded seed pods.

RAT'S-TAIL STATICE
(Psylliostachys suworowii)

These dark to pale pink flowers come in a huge variety of lengths. Although they will be fairly straight when fresh, they tend to drop after a time. They look their best in small bunches and add a distinctive texture to a display.

ROSA PALEANDER

These are the miniature version of the standard dried rose and not generally prone to moth attack. They are available in a huge range of colours. Watch out for the thorns. They look particularly good combined with the larger roses.

ROSES
(Rosa)

One of the most expensive of all dried flowers, they are also the most exquisite. A wide range of different colours is available. Always save them until last so that the rose heads do not get broken and so that they remain most central to your design. Most varieties will welcome a little steaming, which revitalizes them and releases a beautiful scent. Roses are prone to attack from moths and need to be inspected for eggs from time to time.

Pink roses are combined with preserved leaves here to create a warm effect.

Red roses make any arrangement special and are ideal for displays made as gifts.

SANFORDII

Small clusters of bright flowers. The golden yellow colour has a very long life, but the flowerheads need to be supported by other materials or their weight will bend the stems.

SEA HOLLY
(Eryngium)

Clusters of small blue thistles, this is a plant to be handled with gloves! Sea holly has a long life, with the colour lasting a long time. As it fades it becomes grey-green turning to pale brown. *Eryngium alpinum* has purplish-blue, cone-shaped flowerheads and a frilly "collar".

SILENE PENDULA
(Campion)

This tiny pink flower looks as though it is fresh, even when dried. It will lose some petals but not enough to matter. The colour keeps for a long time and you only need to add this flower in small quantities. The small flowerheads create a soft look in a display. Give the flowerheads some support, to stop them hanging down.

SOLIDASTER

A hybrid species made by crossing solidago and aster, this pale yellow flower keeps its colour well. Bunches are fairly large and each stem has dozens of flowers that can be wired into small bunches. A good filler.

STRAWFLOWER
(Helichrysum)

This is one of the best-known dried flowers and has slipped from favour with many arrangers. However, the range of colours is vast and it has a very long life. Used in bunches, it can look quite stunning.

SUNFLOWER
(Helianthus)

These popular large yellow flowers have only recently been added to the list of dried materials. The yellow petals tend to be quite small and to fade, but sunflowers are very good for large extravagant displays. The stems can easily be extended by pushing a cane up into the hollow stem.

TOLBOS
(Top brush)

A spiky form of protea that is becoming more widely available. It has a furry centre and usually bears a number of heads on each stem.

WHEAT

Wheat is only one of a number of grasses available. Although very attractive, these grasses need to be used with care. Unfortunately, their green colour has a very short life, and they have given dried displays a bad reputation as their colour quickly fades to brown.

Strawflowers look striking in small groups and are long-lasting.

EQUIPMENT
· · ·

The flower arranger can get by with the minimum of equipment when he or she is just starting out. However, as he or she becomes more adventurous, a selection of specialized tools and equipment will be useful. This section itemizes those pieces of equipment used in the projects contained in this book.

CANDLE HOLDERS
These plastic fittings are available in a range of sizes. They have a star-shaped base which is easily pushed into dry foam to hold a candle.

CANES
These are used to create a square or triangular frame for a garland.

CHICKEN WIRE
This is a useful base for a swag.

COPPER OR STEEL RINGS
These comprise two thin wire rings, used as a strong base for garlands.

FLORIST'S ADHESIVE
This very sticky glue is supplied in a pot and is the forerunner to the hot, melted adhesive of the glue gun. It is necessary when attaching synthetic ribbons or other materials which might be adversely affected by the heat of a glue gun.

FLORIST'S CLEAR LACQUER
A fixative, specifically for dried materials. It holds loose material in place and also helps to keep it clean.

FLORIST'S SCISSORS
A strong, sharp pair of scissors are the flower arranger's most important tool. As well as cutting all those things you would expect, the scissors must also be sturdy enough to cut woody stems and even wires.

Before starting to build a design make sure you have all the materials close to hand.

FLORIST'S TAPE
(STEM-WRAP TAPE)
This tape is not adhesive, but the heat of your hands will help secure it to itself as it is wrapped around a stem.

The tape is used to conceal wires and seal stem ends. It is made either from plastic or crêpe paper and it will stretch to provide a thin covering. The tape is available in a range of colours, including green.

FLORIST'S WIRE
Wire is used to support, control and secure materials, also to extend stems and to replace them where weight reduction is required. The wire tends to be sold in different lengths. Most of the projects in this book use 35 cm (14 in) lengths. Always use the lightest gauge of wire you can while still providing sufficient support. The most popular gauges are:

1.25mm (18g)	0.28mm (31g)
0.90mm (20g)	0.24mm (32g)
0.71mm (22g)	Silver reel
0.56mm (24g)	*(rose) wires:*
0.46mm (26g)	0.56mm (24g)
0.38mm (28g)	0.32mm (30g)
0.32mm (30g)	0.28mm (32g)

Make sure that the wires are kept in a dry place because any moisture will cause them to rust.

GLOVES
While some flower arranging processes would be impeded by gloves, it makes sense to protect your hands whenever necessary, especially if handling materials with sharp thorns or sap which might irritate the skin. So keep some domestic rubber gloves and heavy-duty gardening gloves in your florist's workbox.

GLUE GUN
The glue gun is an electrically powered device fed by sticks of glue, which it melts to enable the user to apply glue via a trigger action. In floristry it is a relatively recent development but invaluable in allowing the arranger to attach dried or fresh materials to swags, garlands or circlets securely, cleanly and efficiently.

The glue and the tip of the gun are extremely hot, so take care at all times when using a glue gun. Never leave a hot glue gun unattended.

MOSSING (FLORAL) PINS
These are used to hold material, especially moss, in place.

PAPER RIBBON
Paper ribbon is an alternative to satin and synthetic ribbon and is available in a large range of mostly muted, soft colours. It is sold twisted and rolled up. Cut the length of ribbon required in its twisted state and carefully untwist and flatten it to its full width before creating your bow.

PLASTIC FOAM RINGS
Plastic foam rings are lightweight and convenient to handle. Foam for fresh flowers soaks up water very quickly, but must not be resoaked. For dried flowers a softer version of foam is available, so consider which type you need before starting the design.

PLIERS

These are used to secure and twist florist's wires and chicken wire.

RAFFIA

A natural alternative to string and ribbon, raffia has several uses for the flower arranger. It can be used, a few strands at a time, to attach bunches of dried or fresh flowers to garlands and swags, or in thicker swathes it can be used for decorative bows.

ROSE STRIPPER

This ingenious little device is a must when handling very thorny roses. Squeeze the metal claws together and pull the stripper along the stem, and the thorns and leaves will be removed.

The main equipment needed for making wreaths consists of string, reel (rose) wire, florist's tape (stem-wrap tape), florist's wires, a sharp knife, scissors, pliers, a glue gun and spray paint.

There is also a blade attachment to cut stem ends at an angle. Always wear thick gardening gloves.

SATIN RIBBON

Available in a large variety of widths and colours, satin ribbon is invaluable when a final touch to a wreath or garland is required.

Satin ribbon is preferable to synthetic ribbon because it looks and feels so much softer. Its only drawback is that it frays when cut.

SECATEURS (PRUNING SHEARS)

These are necessary to cut the tougher, thicker stems and branches of foliage. Always handle scissors and secateurs with care and do not leave within the reach of young children.

SILVER REEL (ROSE) WIRE

This comes in a range of gauges but it is generally a more delicate wire than florist's wire. Experiment with different thicknesses until you find one with which you like working.

STRING OR TWINE

String or twine is essential for wreaths and garlands. Gardening string comes in various brown and green colours that blend well with floral materials.

TECHNIQUES

. . .

TAPING

Stems and wires are covered with florist's tape (stem-wrap tape) for three reasons: first, cut materials which have been wired can no longer take up water and covering with tape seals in the moisture that already exists in the plant; second, the tape conceals the wires, which are essentially utilitarian, and gives a more natural appearance to the false stem; third, wired dried materials are covered with florist's tape to ensure that the material does not slip out of the wired mount.

1 Hold the wired stem near its top with the end of a length of florist's tape between the thumb and index finger of your left hand (or the opposite way if you are left-handed). With your other hand, hold the remainder of the length of tape at 45° to the wired stem, keeping it taut. Starting at the top of the stem, just above the wires, rotate the flower slowly to wrap the tape around both the stem and wires, working down. By keeping it taut, the tape will stretch into a thin layer around the stem and wires. Each layer should overlap and stick to the one before. You may add flowerheads at different heights as you tape to create units. Finally, fasten off just above the end of the wires by squeezing the tape against itself to stick it securely.

MAKING A STAY WIRE

1 Group together four .71 wires, each overlapping the next by about 3 cm (1¼ in). Start taping the wires together from one end using florist's tape. As the tape reaches the end of the first wire add another .71 wire to the remaining three ends of wire and continue taping, and so on, adding wires and taping four together until you achieve the required length of stay wire.

SINGLE LEG MOUNT

This is for wiring flowers which have a strong natural stem or where a double weight of wire is not necessary to support the material.

1 Hold the flowers or foliage between the thumb and index finger of your left hand (opposite way if you are left-handed) while taking the weight of the material across the top of your hand. Position a wire of the appropriate weight and length

behind the stem about one-third up from the bottom. Bend the wire ends together with one leg shorter than the other. Holding the short wire leg parallel with the stem, wrap the long wire leg firmly around both the stem and the other wire leg several times. Straighten the long wire leg to extend the stem. Cover the stem and wire with florist's tape.

DOUBLE LEG MOUNT

This is formed in the same way as the single leg mount but extends the stem with two equal length wire legs.

1 Hold the flower or foliage between the thumb and index finger of your left hand (or opposite way if you are left-handed) while taking the weight of the plant material across the top of your hand. Position a wire of appropriate weight and length behind the stem about one-third of the way up from the bottom. One-third of the wire should be to one side of the stem with two-thirds to the other. Bend the wire parallel to the stem. One leg will be about twice as long as the other.

Holding the shorter leg against the stem, wrap the longer leg around both stem and the other wire to secure. Straighten both legs which should now be of equal length.

PIPPING

Pipping is the process whereby small flowerheads are removed from a main stem to be wired individually. This process can be used for intricate work with small delicate plant materials.

1 Bend a thin silver wire into a hairpin about its centre and twist at the bend to form a small loop above the two projecting legs.

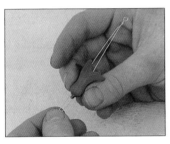

2 Push the legs into the flower centre, down through its throat, and out of its base to create a stem.

3 Using more silver wire, double leg mount this stem with any natural existing stem, and tape if required.

UNITS

A unit is the composite stem formed from two or more pieces of plant material. Units of small flowers can be used in small garlands and candle rings, and units of larger flowers in more substantial wreath designs.

Units should be made up of one type of material only. For small units, first wire and tape the individual flowerheads, buds or leaves.

Start with the smallest of the plant material and attach a slightly larger head to it by taping the wires together. Position the larger head in line with the bottom of the first item. Increase the size of the items as you work downward.

For units of larger flowers you may have to join the wire stems by double leg mounting them with an appropriate weight of wire before taping.

EXTENDING THE LENGTH OF A STEM

Flowerheads with short stems, and flowers that are delicate may need the extra support of an extended stem. There are two methods of extending a stem.

Wire the flowerhead using the appropriate method and correct

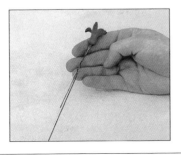

weight of wire. Then single leg mount the wired flowerhead using a .71 wire and tape the wires and any natural stem with florist's tape (stem-wrap tape).

Alternatively, push a .71 wire into the base of the flowerhead from the bottom, then at right angles to this push through a .38 silver wire from one side to the other.

Bend the .38 silver wire so that the two ends point downwards, parallel to the .71 wire. Wrap one leg of .38 wire firmly around its other leg and the .71 wire. Cover with florist's tape (stem-wrap tape).

WIRING AN OPEN FLOWERHEAD

This is a technique for the wiring of individual heads of lily, amaryllis and tulip and is also suitable for small, soft or hollow-stemmed flowers such as anemones and ranunculus.

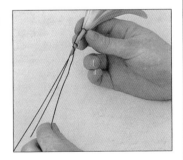

Cut the stem of the flower to around 4 cm (1½ in). Push one .71 wire up through the inside of the stem and into the base of the flowerhead. Double leg mount the stem and its internal wire with a .71 wire. Tape the stem and wire.

The internal wire will add strength to the flower's natural stem and the double leg mount will ensure that the weight of the flowerhead is given sufficient support.

Preserved (dried) apple slices require careful handling when wiring.

WIRING A FRESH ROSE HEAD

Roses have relatively thick, woody stems so to make them suitable for use in intricate work, such as candle rings and headdresses, the natural stem will need to be replaced with a wire stem.

Cut the stem of the rose to a length of approximately 3 cm (1¼ in).

Push one end of a .71 wire through the seed box of the rose at the side. Holding the head of the rose carefully in your left hand (opposite way if left-handed), wrap the wire several times firmly around and down the stem. Straighten the remaining wire to extend the natural stem. Cover the wire and stem with florist's tape (stem-wrap tape).

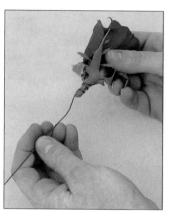

WIRING FRESH FRUIT AND VEGETABLES

Using fruit and vegetables in swags, wreaths and garlands will require wiring them first. The method will depend on the item to be wired and how it is to be used.

Heavy fruits and vegetables, such as oranges, lemons or bulbs of garlic, will need a heavy .71 wire or even .90. The wire should be pushed through the item, just above its base from one side to the other. Push another wire through the item at right angles to the first and bend all four projecting wires to point downwards.

Depending on how the fruit or vegetables will be used, either cut the wires to a suitable length to be pushed into plastic foam, or twist the wires together to form a single stem.

Small delicate fruits and vegetables such as mushrooms or figs need careful handling as their flesh is easily damaged. They normally only need one wire. Push the wire through the

base of the item from one side to the other and bend the two projecting wires downwards. Depending on how the material is to be used, either twist to form a single stem, or trim to push into plastic foam.

For the soft materials .71 is the heaviest weight of wire you will require. In some instances, fruit or vegetables can be attached or secured in an arrangement by pushing a long wire "hairpin" right through the item and into the plastic foam behind.

Fruit or vegetables that have a stem, such as bunches of grapes or artichokes, can be double leg mounted on their stems with appropriate weight wires.

Extend the length of a starfish by double leg mounting one of its legs.

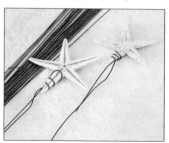

WIRING DRIED FLOWERS

This is the most important skill to master when dealing with dried flowers. Practise on a handful of stems trimmed from a bunch of fresh flowers until you have a neat, tightly wired bunch.

1 Take 4–6 stems and cut them to the length you require. Hold them firmly together with one hand and pass the wire behind them, so that the wire and the stems are at right angles. The short end of the wire should be about 3 cm (1¼ in) above the stems.

2 Hold the wire and stems together between the thumb and forefinger of one hand. Bend the long end of the wire towards you, loop it around the stems and push it away from you.

3 Pull the short end of the wire up so that it lies lengthways along the stems. Now wrap the longer length of wire 3–4 times diagonally around the stems, to hold them together. The wire should be firm but not so tight that it breaks the flower stems.

STEAMING DRIED FLOWERS

This simple technique can greatly improve dried roses or peonies, which are imported in large boxes and often arrive at their destination looking rather squashed. Never try to open the very centre of the flower which is often discoloured.

1 Bring a kettle to the boil. Hold the rose by its stem, head downwards, in the steam for a few seconds, until the outside petals start to waver.

2 Remove the rose from the steam and gently push back the outer petals, one by one. If necessary, repeat the process.

CARE AND MAINTENANCE

How long a display of dried materials will last largely depends on the care that it receives. Avoid direct sunlight and keep your display in a dry and damp-free atmosphere and it should last at least one or two years.

After about a year, your display will need cleaning. Set an electric hairdryer on cold and move it backwards and forwards over the display. Use a small paintbrush to clean away dust also. Remove any bits that are old or broken. Spray florist's sealer on your display for a further lift. Frosted spray paints can also transform a display that is too old to revive.

WIRING DRIED LEAVES

Leaves such as magnolia often arrive with little or no stem. This technique creates a stem to work with so that you can make bunches. Be careful not to trim away more of the leaf than is necessary; just enough to fix the wire.

1 Trim the bottom third of the leaf away on one side of the stalk and repeat on the other side, to leave a thick long stem. Bunch the leaves together and centre-wire. For a full look, alter the angle of each leaf.

WIRING DRIED FRUIT AND NUTS

Many fruits can be wired easily but nuts need to be drilled or make a hole very carefully with a bradawl (awl). It is advisable to hold the nut in a vice. You can also use a glue gun to fix fruit or nuts directly in place.

1 If necessary, make a hole through the base of the fruit or nut. Push a wire through so that an even amount of wire comes out either side.

2 Cross the two ends of the wire and twist them together to form a strong support.

Preparing a Copper or Steel Garland Ring

Copper or steel rings are a strong and inexpensive way of creating a good base for garlands. They are available in a large range of sizes and need to be covered in moss or hay.

1 Tie silver reel (rose) wire to one of the copper wires of the ring. Take a good handful of moss or hay and hold it on to both the top and the bottom of the ring, to form an even layer. Wrap the wire around the ring, fixing the moss or hay in place. Repeat all the way round the ring.

Covering a Picture or Mirror Frame with a Chicken Wire Swag

A picture or mirror frame can be covered with moss as the base for a dried flower arrangement. The best base is a simple, heavy frame.

1 If the frame is a little flimsy, use wood screws and glue to strengthen it. Make four chicken wire and moss swags to fit the top, bottom and sides. Push one swag firmly around one side of the picture frame and make sure that it is long enough.

2 Use a staple gun to hold the swag in place. Make sure that the staples trap a piece of chicken wire and hold it firmly to the wooden frame each time you fire the gun. Repeat every 5–7.5 cm (2–3 in).

Making a Chicken Wire Swag

This method of creating a swag base makes a large surface to work with, useful if your materials are chunky or you need to cover a large area.

1 Carefully cut the required length and width of chicken wire, folding in the sharp edges.

2 Fill the centre of the wire mesh along its length with moss, as evenly as possible.

3 Fold the long edges into each other, creating a sausage shape, and join them together with short wires. You may need to remove or add moss, so that the shape is even along its length.

4 Use one or two short wires to make a hanger. Push the wire(s) through the chicken wire and twist the ends together to create a loop.

Making a Rope Swag

This is the best base for a swag to which you are going to tie the decorative materials. The covering need not be too thick; the bulk for the swag will be provided by the stems of the materials. Don't be tempted to make the swag too short – a swag about 1 m (1 yd) long will look balanced in most projects.

1 Cut the rope to the required length, allowing enough for a loop at each end. Use wire or glue to secure the loops.

2 Tie silver reel (rose) wire to the rope and wrap it around a good handful of moss, keeping the rope in the centre of the moss. Work along the whole length of the rope until it is completely covered with moss.

MAKING A BASKET BORDER WITH A ROPE SWAG

You can use a moss-covered rope swag to extend the edge of a basket, making it easier to fix materials in position.

1 Make a rope swag as above. Attach the rope to the edge of the basket by pushing wires through the basket under the rope. Twist the ends together on top, trim off the loose ends and push any sharp pieces back into the moss. Repeat every 5–7.5 cm (2–3 in) round the edge of the basket.

MAKING A HAY ROPE OR COLLAR

Hay is inexpensive and versatile, so it is well worth mastering this basic technique, used for garlands and swags.

1 Take a good handful of hay and scrunch it up to form a sausage. Wind silver reel (rose) wire (or string or raffia) around this and tie in place. Twist the wire round the hay, leaving spaces of about 1 cm (½ in) between each twist. Keep adding more hay as you build up the length of rope.

2 Add more hay, packing it firmly and keeping the width of the rope even, until you reach the required length. If you are making a rope for a swag, it need only be about 5 mm (¼ in) in diameter. For a garland or a very large swag, the diameter needs to be about 2.5 cm (1 in).

WIRING A CANDLE

This method firmly fixes a candle into foam, and makes removing the spent candle very easy.

The combination of candles and dried material is, of course, potentially very dangerous. Make sure that you never leave a display with a lighted candle unattended.

1 Wrap florist's tape (stem-wrap tape) at least once around the base of the candle, so that it sticks firmly to the candle.

2 Place a mossing (floral) pin or a short bent wire under the loose end of the tape. Cover the top of the pin or wire with the tape so that it holds the pin or wire in place.

3 Repeat with at least three fixings for a small candle or six for a larger candle. Finish by pulling the tape around once more and trimming it neatly. Alternatively, you could use a glue gun to fix the candle in the right position.

MAKING A FABRIC BOW

For a more formal setting, a fabric bow looks smart. Crinkled paper can be used for a quicker and more inexpensive method.

1 Fold a piece of fabric equally into three lengthways, making sure that the raw edge is not too close to one of the folded edges. Fold the length again, dividing it into three so that the middle section is approximately one-third larger than the outer two.

2 Grip the fabric in the middle, pressing it into a bow shape. Still holding the shape, wrap a thin wire around it and twist the ends together. Make sure that the creases on the front of the bow are even. Twist the wires tightly together with pliers and tuck the sharp ends into the bow.

3 Fold a much smaller piece of fabric into three lengthways. It should be wide enough to look well balanced as the centre of the bow. Wrap this around the bow, covering the wire. Trim the ends at the back then glue the two raw ends together.

WREATHS AND
GARLANDS

* * *

*From a simple garland of natural-coloured twigs
to the most extravagant gilded spice wreath, here
you will find fresh and dried wreaths and garlands
to suit every colour scheme and every occasion.*

INTRODUCTION

· · ·

Above: Herb and Dried Fruits Wreath

Below: Lavender and Seagrass Wreath

Wreaths and garlands are among the most impressive of displays, whether hung indoors in the kitchen, living room or bedroom, or used outside to adorn a front door or gate.

Simple wreaths and garlands decorated with roses, lavender and herbs are a great way to bring the colours and scents of nature into your home, and more unusual garlands can be made using a single dramatic dried material such as massed dahlia heads, giant sunflowers or even wild barley, to create a very modern look. In fact, there is no limit to the number of designs that are possible and the projects in this chapter range from fresh roses with Queen Anne's lace to beautifully scented herbal wreaths made from bay leaves, rosemary, marjoram and mint, and even a vegetable garden wreath made with carrots and turnips.

One of the most popular materials for making wreaths and garlands is lavender, both for its wonderful colour and of course for its aroma, and this material features in several projects in this chapter. Lavender is an important plant in the traditional cottage garden and has been widely cultivated over centuries for the perfume of its purple flowers. Its healing powers are used in aromatherapy to ease headaches and stress, and a wreath made of lavender will fill any room in which it hangs with the rich scent of summer. In this chapter you will find out how to make a fresh

Above: Wild Barley Garland

Left: Midsummer Hay Wreath

lavender wreath mixed with herbs, and dried lavender wreaths bundled together with roses, strawflowers, cornflowers or even dried fruit. For a really striking but easy-to-make display, there is a dried wreath made of massed lavender sprigs tied with natural seagrass rope.

Roses are another very popular material, and can be used either fresh or dried in wreaths and garlands. When dried, remember that they can be quite fragile; keep them away from strong sunlight, dust them gently and periodically add a few drops of essential oil to keep them perfumed.

Whatever the finished design, all wreaths and garlands are built on a base, which you can buy from a florist's or make yourself. Ready-made rings woven from natural materials such as hop vine or willow are available from florists in many different sizes. If you like the idea of weaving your own ring, use vines or twigs cut when they are green so that they are pliable. Leave the ring to dry out naturally before adding the decoration. You can make your own hay ring by binding the hay with silver reel (rose) wire. Another, more expensive base is a copper or steel ring, which consists of two wire circles. This can be covered with hay or moss, or in some garland designs one of the wire circles is used on its own.

Remember that the material lists are only a guide: don't be afraid to experiment with other flower and colour combinations and, in time, to create your own original designs.

Below: Sweet Herb Wreath

FRESH HERBAL WREATH

· · ·

· · ·

*30 cm (12 in) plastic foam
wreath frame*

· · ·

scissors

· · ·

2 branches bay leaves

· · ·

2 bunches rosemary

· · ·

.71 wires

· · ·

6 large bulbs (heads) garlic

· · ·

6 or 7 beetroot (beets)

· · ·

*40 stems flowering
marjoram*

· · ·

40 stems flowering mint

*As well as being decorative, a
herb wreath can also be useful.
The herbs can be taken from it
and used in the kitchen
without causing too much
damage to the overall design.*

In many parts of Europe it is believed that a herb wreath hung in a kitchen, or by the entrance of a house, is a sign of welcome, wealth and good luck. This wreath will stay fresh for two or three weeks because the stems of the herbs are in water, but even if it dries out it will continue to look good for some time.

1 Soak the wreath frame thoroughly in cold water. Create the background by making a foliage outline using evenly distributed bay leaves and sprigs of rosemary. To ensure an even covering, position the leaves inside, on top and on the outside of the wreath frame.

2 Wire the garlic bulbs (heads) and beetroot (beets) by pushing two wires through their base so that they cross, then pull the projecting wires down and cut to the correct length for the depth of the foam. Decide where on the wreath they are to be positioned and push the wires firmly into the foam.

3 Infill the spaces in the wreath, concentrating the marjoram around the beetroot and the mint around the garlic.

SWEET HERB WREATH
. . .

MATERIALS
. . .
silver reel (rose) wire
. . .
sage
. . .
fresh or dried lavender
. . .
parsley
. . .
glue gun and glue sticks
. . .
*30 cm (12 in) diameter cane
wreath base*
. . .
chives
. . .
scissors
. . .
raffia

*Generous raffia ties look great
around thick bunches of chives.*

Sweet-smelling herbs make a lovely decoration, trimmed with casually tied strands of raffia. Individual bunches of sage, lavender and parsley are overlapped around the wreath base to cover the stems and give a rich, full effect. Criss-cross bunches of chives are then added on top. The fresh herbs will not last long but you can take the wreath apart and hang up the separate bunches of herbs to dry.

1 Using silver reel (rose) wire, bind the sage, lavender and parsley into generous bunches. Using a glue gun, fix two bunches of sage to the wreath base, with the stems pointing inwards.

2 Attach enough lavender bunches side by side to cover the width of the wreath base, hiding the sage stems. Attach bunches of parsley to cover the lavender stems in the same way. Continue around the wreath base, alternating these three herbs, until it is entirely covered.

3 Wire the chives into four generous bunches and trim the cut ends straight. Form the bunches into crosses as shown and bind with raffia. Bind the two chive crosses on to the wreath with wire.

4 Tie raffia around the wreath at intervals. Make a raffia hanging loop and thread it on to a bundle of raffia at the top of the wreath. Tie the ends into a bow.

GLORIOUS SUMMER
WREATH
• • •

MATERIALS

• • •

plastic foam ring

• • •

secateurs (pruning shears)

• • •

pale pink roses

• • •

Queen Anne's lace

• • •

a few wild roses

• • •

plant spray

*Queen Anne's lace makes an
exquisite contrast with the
creamy-smooth petals of
the roses.*

In early summer the countryside is covered with the frothy, creamy white flowers of Queen Anne's lace, or cow parsley. Gathered in the fields, it makes a perfect accompaniment to pale pink garden roses, which are in bloom at the same time.

1 Immerse the plastic foam ring in water for up to half an hour, until thoroughly soaked. Trim the rose stems to about 2.5 cm (1 in).

2 Push the rose stems into the foam ring, angling the heads to create an attractive design. Fill in the gaps between the roses with sprigs of Queen Anne's lace until the foam base is completely covered.

3 Add a few wild roses, placing them carefully so they are not hidden by the other flowers. Spray the finished wreath well with water.

EUCALYPTUS WREATH
. . .

MATERIALS
. . .
wire-cutters
. . .
garden wire
. . .
florist's tape (stem-wrap tape)
. . .
*heavy-gauge silver reel (rose)
wire*
. . .
large bunch of eucalyptus

*Eucalyptus is ideal for using
in a fresh wreath because it is
very strong, but still flexible.*

Subtle blue-green eucalyptus makes a simple wreath that will dry naturally to
give a long-lasting decoration. There are many different varieties of
eucalyptus, with round or oval leaves and with a lovely fresh scent. The wreath is
very easy to make, using strands of thick garden wire to make a circular base, and
the sturdy eucalyptus branches are quite pliable and easy to work with.

1 Using three strands of garden wire, make
a circle about 35 cm (14 in) in diameter
and bind with florist's tape (stem-wrap
tape). Using silver reel (rose) wire, bind a
small piece of eucalyptus to the ring.

2 Wire the other end of the stem to
the ring. Add another branch
of eucalyptus, again wiring it at top
and bottom.

3 Add extra branches to
fill out the wreath.
Continue in this way all
around the wire ring until
the wreath is complete and
looks rich and lush.

COUNTRY FLOWER WREATH
. . .

MATERIALS
. . .

scissors

. . .

florist's scissors

. . .

green binding twine

. . .

grass stems

. . .

green twine

. . .

selection of small, colourful flowers (eg marigolds, cornflowers, spray chrysanthemums, roses, irises)

. . .

small-leafed foliage (eg box)

. . .

silver reel (rose) wire

A flower ring displayed on a door or gate might be used to signal a warm welcome to party guests.

In Greece there is a lovely custom in which a colourful floral wreath, or *stefani*, is hung on the front door. The wreaths are made very simply of grass stems bound with twine and decorated with wild and garden flowers. If the grass stems you collect are too stiff to bend into a circle, soak them in water and hang them up in a bunch to dry.

1 In the Greek tradition, the ring is composed of flower posies selected and arranged at random, not carefully matched and arranged symmetrically. Try to include some wild flowers if available. If the stems you cut to make the ring are too rigid to shape into a circle, soak them in water, then hang them in a bunch to dry.

3 Sort the flowers into groups, those which will be bound into posies and others which will be added individually. Mix and match the flowers for the posies to give the most colourful and informal effect. Cut short the stems of the posy flowers and foliage and bind with silver reel (rose) wire.

2 Cut the grass stems to the length you require. This ring is 30 cm (12 in) in diameter, made of stems 100 cm (40 in) long. Gather them into a neat bundle and pull out any which are particularly wayward. Wrap the twine around the stems, tie it in a knot, then bind it around them, adding more grass as you proceed. Overlap the stem ends to form a circle and bind securely. Tie the twine in a knot and cut off the end.

4 Using twine or wire, bind on the flower posies and the individual flowers, so that the heads of each posy or flower head cover the stems and binding of the one before. It is not necessary to conceal all the grass ring since it is a natural part of the design.

ROSEHIP WREATH

. . .

MATERIALS
. . .
silver reel (rose) wire
. . .
trailing stems of rosehips
. . .
secateurs (pruning shears)

Varieties of roses that have attractive glossy rosehips like these should not be dead-headed in the summer if you want the hips to develop.

Make an enchantingly wild-looking wreath using tough, leafy stems studded with bright orange or scarlet rosehips. Climbing and rambling roses produce long, trailing branches that can be twined around into a circle, carefully avoiding the sharp thorns. The brilliantly coloured rosehip wreath looks its best on a rustic wooden door.

1 Using silver reel (rose) wire, bind together the ends of two long stems of rosehips.

2 Bind the other two ends together to make a circle. If necessary, use three stems to make up the circle.

3 Add more stems where the wreath needs extra fullness. Twist them into the main circle.

LAVENDER AND SEAGRASS WREATH

• • •

MATERIALS

• • •

wire-cutters

• • •

garden wire

• • •

silver reel (rose) wire

• • •

lavender

• • •

green raffia

• • •

scissors

• • •

natural seagrass rope or coarse string

Freshly picked stalks of lavender are pliable and easy to work with, and look wonderful bound with natural seagrass rope.

Massed on its own, lavender always looks wonderful as the beautiful colour of the small flowers is intensified. The fragrant lavender flowers can be any shade of mauve, blue or dark purple, even white, and should last all year long.

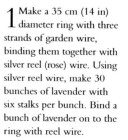

1 Make a 35 cm (14 in) diameter ring with three strands of garden wire, binding them together with silver reel (rose) wire. Using silver reel wire, make 30 bunches of lavender with six stalks per bunch. Bind a bunch of lavender on to the ring with reel wire.

2 Continue to bind more lavender bunches around the ring, packing them closely together.

3 When the ring is covered add extra bunches of lavender, tying them in place with green raffia to hide any garden wire that is still visible. Wind seagrass rope or string around the wreath and tie the ends in a large bow.

DRIED AROMATIC WREATH

. . .

The sweet scents of marjoram and lavender combine in this pretty ring, which is very simple to make. Accentuate the natural pinks and mauve-blues of the tiny flowers with coloured string, using it to bind the bunches of herbs on to the willow wreath base. You will need twice as much lavender as marjoram to give a nicely balanced effect. Being made entirely of dried flowers, the wreath will last well.

MATERIALS

. . .

.71 florist's wires

. . .

dried lavender

. . .

dried marjoram

. . .

38 cm (15 in) diameter willow
wreath base

. . .

deep pink and blue string

. . .

scissors

The bands of alternating herbs lend impact to this easy-to-make wreath.

1 Using florist's wires, wire the lavender into bunches. Repeat with the marjoram.

2 Place a row of marjoram bunches across the width of the wreath and tie in position with deep pink string. Lay a row of lavender bunches just below the marjoram and tie them on with blue string. Repeat, alternating the marjoram and lavender, until the whole wreath is covered.

DRIED LAVENDER WREATH

· · ·

If you have a plentiful source of lavender, this sturdy wreath is a variation on the traditional theme of delicate lavender garlands. It is made using the florist's technique of spiral-binding, wrapping the seagrass rope around the stalks to bind them to the twig base – it doesn't matter if some of the twigs show through. Once made, this wreath will last for years and fill the room in which it hangs with the scent of lazy summer afternoons.

Seagrass rope has a lovely, natural texture that goes perfectly with dried lavender.

1 Tie one end of the rope securely to the twig wreath base.

2 Take a handful of lavender stalks and with one hand hold it across the wreath, with the flowers pointing outwards. Hold the rope in the other hand and wind it around the stalks, then over the wreath to bind the stalks in place.

3 Place a second bunch of lavender to the right of the first and bind in place, wrapping the rope once or twice around the stalks to secure them. Place the next bunch to the right of the second, with the flowers pointing away from the wreath.

4 Continue to spiral-bind small bunches in the same way. When the ring is completely covered, tie off the end of the rope securely, and make a loop for hanging.

OLD-FASHIONED GARLAND

· · ·

*Make the posies using an
assortment of colourful and
fragrant old-fashioned flowers.*

Posies of dried flowers and sweet-scented lavender make a very pretty traditional garland, decorated with bows of satin ribbon. Hang the garland on a bedroom wall, or alternatively lay it flat on a table, window seat or linen chest. Made up in a smaller size, it would make a lovely, long-lasting gift to hang in a wardrobe.

1 For the posies which are to alternate with the lavender bunches, choose flowers in soft, complementary colours – blue, cream, and green are ideal. If a hot-glue gun is not available, the bunches and posies can be fixed to the wreath form with stub wires bent into U-shaped staples.

2 Gather eight to ten lavender stalks into a bunch, cut short the stalks and bind them with silver reel (rose) wire. Make mixed posies with the other dried flowers, arranging full, rounded flowers such as roses and cornflowers in the centre and wispy sprays at the sides.

3 Spread a thin strip of glue along the stems of the first bunch of lavender. Press it on to the twig wreath base, holding it in place for a second or so while the glue sets. Stick on more bunches, the heads of each successive bunch covering the stalks of the one before. Continue around the ring, spacing the lavender and posies as desired.

4 Cut six equal lengths of ribbon. Tie each length into a bow and trim the ends. Cut the florist's wires in half and bend them to make U-shaped staples. Press five ribbon bows into the inside of the wreath base and one on top. Adjust the ribbons so that they hang neatly and evenly. Glue on extra strawflower heads if there are any gaps or wires visible.

DRIED ROSE WREATH
· · ·

dried red rosebuds

· · ·

dried cream rosebuds

· · ·

paper-covered wire plant twists

· · ·

scissors

· · ·

loosely woven ring of twigs

· · ·

dried lavender

· · ·

dried hydrangea heads

· · ·

essential rose oil

· · ·

red ribbon

The materials in this dried floral wreath will look wonderful as a wall-hanging.

M any flowers, including roses, dry beautifully and can be enjoyed for months after fresh flowers would have perished. Kept away from strong sunlight, which will fade the petals, dried flowers need gentle dusting and a few drops of essential oils to keep them perfumed. As dried flowers are very fragile and easily broken, a wall-hanging wreath is an ideal way of arranging them and makes a country-style alternative to a picture.

1 Divide the rosebuds into five bunches and tie with the plant twists. Cut the the stems to 5 cm (2 in) and use the ends of the plant twists to attach the bunches to the wreath. Repeat with the lavender.

2 Tie the hydrangea heads to the ring of twigs using the wire twists so that they conceal any stems and cover the twigs. Add just a few drops of essential rose oil.

3 Attach the ribbon firmly with a bow and use it to loop the wreath over a picture hook. Refresh with essential oil when it loses its scent and dust carefully from time to time.

HYDRANGEA CIRCLET
· · ·

Hydrangea heads remain beautiful when dried but they do not necessarily dry well when hung in the air. Thus, while it might seem a contradiction in terms, it is best to dry hydrangea whilst they are standing in shallow water. This slows down the process and avoids the hydrangea florets shrivelling.

There is an enormous range of hydrangea colours, from white through pinks, greens, blues and reds to deep purples and in most cases they keep these colours when dried so are ideal for dried flower arranging.

MATERIALS
· · ·
12 full dried heads hydrangea
· · ·
scissors
· · ·
.71 wire
· · ·
.32 silver reel (rose) wire
· · ·
1 vine circlet, about 35 cm (14 in) diameter

1 Break down each hydrangea head into five smaller florets. Double leg mount each one individually with .71 wire.

This circlet is a celebration of the colours of dried hydrangeas and the soft, almost watercolour, look of these hues makes it the perfect decoration for the wall of a bedroom.

2 Take a long length of .32 silver reel (rose) wire and attach a hydrangea floret to the vine circlet by stitching the wire around one of the vines and the wired stem of the hydrangea, pulling tight to secure. Using the same continuous length of wire, add consecutive hydrangea florets in the same way, slightly overlapping them until the front surface of the vine surface is covered.

3 Finish by stitching the silver reel (rose) wire several times around the vine.

VEGETABLE GARDEN WREATH

· · ·

MATERIALS

· · ·

sprigs of sage

· · ·

*medium-gauge silver reel
(rose) wire*

· · ·

secateurs (pruning shears)

· · ·

20 miniature carrots

· · ·

10 miniature turnips

· · ·

green raffia

· · ·

*40 cm (16 in) diameter willow
wreath base*

*Hang this vegetable wreath
on a kitchen wall or in
the conservatory for a
summer party.*

Celebrate the soft grey-green colours of aromatic sage leaves by using them on their own to cover a willow wreath base. Tiny bunches of miniature carrots and turnips, tied with green raffia, make a charming and witty decorative detail. Sage wilts quite quickly so make up the wreath at the last minute or, alternatively, place the sage-covered wreath in a bowl of water until needed.

1 Bind the sage leaves into small bunches, using silver reel (rose) wire. Put the bunches into water as you make them.

2 Tie the carrots and turnips into bunches of two or three, using green raffia.

3 Wire the sage bunches on to the wreath base at the last minute. Alternatively, wire the sage on to the wreath, then lay it in a basin of water until it is time to put it on display.

4 Wind wire around the bunches of miniature vegetables and use this to attach them to the wreath.

HERB AND DRIED FRUITS WREATH

· · ·

Rosemary, lavender and oranges make a heady combination in this sweet-smelling wreath.

Rosemary and lavender provide two of the most popular essential oils used in aromatherapy, and the citrus scent of the dried orange slices is released when they are threaded on to wires. As the fragrance of the fresh herbs in this wreath begins to fade, it can be refreshed with a couple of drops of essential oil.

1 Divide the rosemary into sprigs approximately 15 cm (6 in) long, using secateurs (pruning shears). Tie one end of the raffia to the wreath and bind the rosemary sprigs to the top and sides.

2 Thread two or three slices of dried orange on to a florist's wire, leaving enough wire at either end to bind around the wreath. Repeat to make five groups.

3 Using raffia, tie the stems of lavender together in groups of eight to ten to make tiny posies approximately 5 cm (2 in) long.

4 Space the orange slices evenly around the ring, then take the wire around the sides and twist the two ends together at the back of the wreath. The wire will also help to keep the rosemary firmly in place.

5 Position the lavender bunches between the groups of orange slices, so that the flower heads follow the line of the rosemary sprigs. Secure them firmly with raffia.

6 Cut the stems off the poppy seed heads. Give the base of each seed head a generous blob of glue, and immediately press it on to the wreath wherever there is a space around the orange slices or to conceal any wire. Decide which way up the wreath looks best and tie a raffia hanging loop to the top.

ROSE AND POT-POURRI GARLAND
• • •

MATERIALS
. . .
dried roses
. . .
scissors
. . .
glue gun and glue sticks
. . .
hop vine ring
. . .
moss
. . .
pot-pourri
. . .
small fir cones or woody material
. . .
raffia

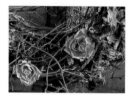

Keep the decoration of this garland light and delicate.

This pretty garland uses a hop vine ring as its base. These are fairly inexpensive and can be purchased from most florists. If you prefer to make your own ring, use vines or twigs cut when green so that they are pliable. Weave them together into a circle then leave to dry completely.

1 Steam the roses if necessary (see Techniques). Cut off the stems and glue the heads to the ring, some in pairs and others as single roses to achieve a good balance. Glue moss in the gaps between the roses.

2 Apply generous quantities of glue directly on to the ring. Sprinkle on pot-pourri to cover the glue completely. Finally, add the fir cones. Tie strands of raffia in a trailing bow and glue to the top of the garland.

ROMANTIC HERB GARLAND

· · ·

Mix herbs and flowers to create a sweet-smelling garland for a wall or table centrepiece. This design is made using a simple hay ring base, which you can make yourself. Divide the ring into sections and add the dried material evenly to make sure you end up with a nicely balanced effect.

MATERIALS

· · ·

dried herbs and flowers,
e.g. Achillea ptarmica,
bay leaves, lavender,
marjoram, mint, poppy
seed heads, oregano

· · ·

scissors

· · ·

silver reel (rose) wire

· · ·

hay-covered copper garland
ring (see Techniques)

The Achillea ptarmica *adds splashes of white to the display, which contrast nicely against the green herbs.*

1 Separate the dried materials and trim the stems to equal length. Wire 4–6 stems at a time to the hay ring, winding the wire around to hold them in place. Continue until you have covered the whole hay ring.

2 Cut the end of the wire and tuck it neatly into the ring.

GIANT SUNFLOWER GARLAND

· · ·

MATERIALS

· · ·

large hay-covered copper garland ring (see Techniques)

· · ·

strong florist's wire

· · ·

dried materials, e.g. Alchemilla mollis, amaranthus, blue larkspur, carthamus, eucalyptus, nigella, twigs

· · ·

scissors

· · ·

silver reel (rose) wire

· · ·

dried sunflowers

· · ·

.91 wires

The large size of this garland is in proportion to the giant sunflowers.

This wonderfully flamboyant garland celebrates the vivid colour and dramatic shape of sunflowers. Attach all of the sunflower heads as low down their stems as possible so that they stand proud of the other material – you should be able to push your fingers easily around each flower. The other materials provide a range of other bright colours which contrast nicely with the yellow of the sunflowers.

1 To make a loop for hanging the finished garland, bend a strong wire into a U-shape. Push it through the hay ring as shown.

2 Check the size of the loop and adjust it by pulling or pushing the wire through the hay to make the loop larger or smaller.

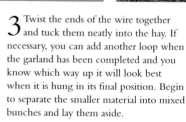

3 Twist the ends of the wire together and tuck them neatly into the hay. If necessary, you can add another loop when the garland has been completed and you know which way up it will look best when it is hung in its final position. Begin to separate the smaller material into mixed bunches and lay them aside.

4 Trim the stems of the smaller bunches to about 20 cm (8 in). Lay them in position and wind around silver reel (rose) wire to bind the stems tightly to the ring.

5 Wire the sunflowers (see Techniques). Push the wired stems through the ring from the front then twist the wire ends and tuck into the back. Fill small gaps with small bunches of material.

Use this large garland to decorate a door or window.

WHITE DAHLIA GARLAND
• • •

MATERIALS
• • •
silver reel (rose) wire
• • •
large wicker garland base
• • •
moss
• • •
scissors
• • •
glue gun and glue sticks
• • •
dried white dahlia heads
• • •
sea-grass rope

The starkness of using all creamy-white flowers is quite eye-catching.

Large, creamy-white dahlia flowers make a stunning garland, loosely looped with bleached rope for a fresh summer feeling. Trim the stems before you start so the flowerheads can be glued directly on to the base.

1 Attach one end of the silver reel (rose) wire to the outside edge of the garland base and tie securely.

2 Add layers of moss on to the top of the garland base. Wind the reel (rose) wire around the base to secure the moss.

3 Continue to add the moss until the whole garland base has been covered. Cut the wire and tie securely.

4 Squeeze some glue on to the underside of a dahlia head and press it firmly on to the moss-covered garland. Continue, leaving no gaps. Overlap the flowerheads if necessary.

5 Continue until the whole garland is covered. Place the flowers deep into the inner ring, and as far down the outer edge as possible.

6 Attach a length of sea-grass rope to the outer edge of the underside of the garland base. Tie in a secure knot and trim the end.

Massing together one flower creates a sumptuous effect. You could make the same design using bright red or yellow dahlias for quite a different look.

7 Wind the rope loosely over the garland. Taking care not to damage the flowers, position it diagonally at regular intervals around the circle.

8 Turn the garland over and make a substantial hanging loop in the rope. Tie a secure knot quite low down where it will not be seen.

9 To finish, wind the end of the rope around the base of the hanging loop several times in a neat spiral then tuck it into the back of the garland.

LAVENDER AND HERB GARLAND

· · ·

MATERIALS

· · ·

scissors

· · ·

.91 wires

· · ·

dried lavender

· · ·

dried artemisia

· · ·

dried lovage

· · ·

dried tarragon

· · ·

glue gun and glue sticks

· · ·

small wicker garland base

· · ·

dried French lavender

Sweet-smelling herbs and flowers are always a delight to work with, and they make the finished garland very fresh and summery.

This pretty garland is composed of mixed herbs and two kinds of lavender, all of which are highly scented. French lavender has large flowerheads, so place these individually at the end to stand out against the smaller-flowered materials.

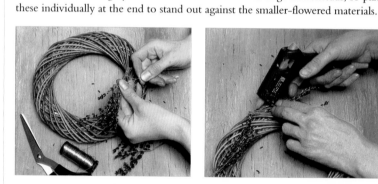

1 Trim and wire all the dried herbs and flowers, except the French lavender, into small bunches.

2 Using a glue gun, glue the first bunch of the dried lavender neatly on to the garland base.

3 Next glue a bunch of artemisia to the garland base between the lavender.

4 Work around the garland, adding a bunch of lovage.

5 Continue all round the garland, interspersing the different bunches of herbs to cover it completely.

6 Finally, add the individual French lavender flowerheads, positioning them regularly around the garland.

MOSS AND TWIG WREATH
· · ·

MATERIALS
· · ·
wire-cutters
· · ·
*strong garden wire, for hanging
the wreath*
· · ·
*30 cm (12 in) diameter straw
wreath base*
· · ·
carpet moss
· · ·
wire pins
· · ·
*other mosses (eg oak moss,
Spanish moss, reindeer moss,
bun moss)*
· · ·
glue gun and glue sticks
· · ·
small, open fir cones
· · ·
.91 florist's wires
· · ·
golden mushrooms
· · ·
twigs

*Mushrooms add the finishing
touch to this mossy wreath.*

Country materials make a fascinating textured wreath in subtle shades of green and brown. Fallen fir cones and twigs can be collected on a winter's walk and the other materials are available from florist's suppliers. Tear the carpet moss rather than cutting it so that the pieces join up in a natural-looking way.

1 Attach a loop of wire to the back of the wreath. Cover the ring with carpet moss, pinning it as you go, until covered. Start to position the other mosses, also pinning them.

2 Alternatively, glue the decorative mosses in place using a glue gun.

3 Join pairs of fir cones together by twisting a piece of florist's wire between the scales at the base of each cone. Apply glue to the base of the fir cones and press them on to the wreath.

4 Place the golden mushrooms evenly around the wreath and glue securely in place. Using wire pins, add small groups of twigs.

TWIGGY WREATH
· · ·

MATERIALS
· · ·

*strong scissors or secateurs
(pruning shears)*

· · ·

thin hazel branches

· · ·

*heavy-gauge silver reel
(rose) wire*

· · ·

short twiggy prunings

*This wreath is made of
young hazel, but you can
use any other twiggy
prunings you can find.*

Asimple, unadorned hazel twig wreath has great character and would look wonderful displayed indoors or outdoors on a wall or door. It is easiest to work with the twigs while they are still fresh and flexible; hazel twigs with catkins attached are very attractive but you can equally well use other twiggy prunings. Check the wreath as you work to keep a full, even shape.

1 Bend half of the longer branches with your hands to make a curved shape. Bend the same number of longer branches in the opposite direction. Place the two sets of curved branches so that they form a circle, overlapping the ends. Bind together with silver reel (rose) wire.

2 Take a bunch of short twiggy prunings and hold firmly in one hand at the top of the circle. Using your other hand, wrap the reel wire around both the prunings and the circle to join them together. Pull the wire tight.

3 Continue with the same length of wire, adding more bunches of prunings until the circle is covered. Check as you work that the wreath looks even.

4 Cut the wire and wrap round the wreath to secure the end. Poke extra prunings into the wreath to give it more texture and hide the wire.

WILD BARLEY GARLAND

· · ·

Search any patch of long grass in late spring and you'll find wild barley growing in abundance.

Overlapping bundles of golden barley create a lovely swirling shape in this simple garland, which uses florist's tape (stem-wrap tape) to bind the stalks to a ring of garden wire. In the summer, barley is often found growing wild in the countryside, and even on open ground in towns and cities. The colour deepens from pale green to deep gold as the season progresses.

1 Make a circle about 18 cm (7 in) in diameter, using several strands of wire. Bind it all the way round with florist's tape (stem-wrap tape).

2 Make bundles of six ears of barley, cutting the stems to about 5 cm (2 in) long, and bind securely with the florist's tape.

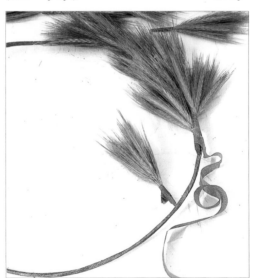

3 Bind the first bundle to the outside of the wire ring with tape. Place the next bundle on the inside of the ring, overlapping the stems of the first bundle, and bind. Place the third bundle on the outside of the wire, overlapping the second, and bind. Continue in this way until the ring is covered completely.

MIDSUMMER HAY WREATH

· · ·

MATERIALS
· · ·
green twine
· · ·
double-circle copper wire ring
· · ·
dry hay
· · ·
scissors
· · ·
selection of dried flowers (eg sea lavender, statice, cornflowers, orange strawflowers, carthamus)
· · ·
silver reel (rose) wire
· · ·
wire-cutters
· · ·
.71 florist's wires
· · ·
1.5 cm (½ in) wide ribbons, in toning colours

The brighter the flowers the better in this rainbow-coloured summer wreath.

Celebrate summer with an exuberant wreath decorated with brightly coloured dried flowers. The best base to use is a 'dished' type of double-circle ring, in which the inner circle is slightly lower than the outer one. Cover this with hay, simply bound on with twine, then decorate gaily with flowers and ribbons. Fill the whole wreath with flowers or leave part of the hay uncovered.

1 Tie the twine to the outer circle of the wire ring. Take a handful of hay and place it over the ring, then bind it on securely, taking the twine over and through the ring. Pull the twine tightly so that it is concealed in the hay. Continue in this way until the ring is completely covered, then cut the twine and tie it to the ring.

2 Gather the flowers into small posies, mixing the colours to give the brightest effect. Use plenty of bright blue cornflowers and orange strawflowers. Cut the stalks short, then bind them with silver reel (rose) wire.

3 Cut several florist's wires in half and bend to make U-shaped pins. Place a posy on the hay-covered ring, loop a wire pin over the stalks, then press it firmly into the hay. Bend back the ends of the wire and twist them around the back of the ring to secure.

4 Add more posies around the ring, placing them so that the heads of each posy cover the stalks of the one before. Leave part of the hay uncovered if you wish. Cut equal lengths of each ribbon. Fold them in half, twist a U-shaped wire pin around the centre and push it into the wreath.

DRIED GRASS GARLAND

· · ·

MATERIALS

· · ·

pliers

· · ·

1 m (1 yd) garden wire

· · ·

scissors

· · ·

florist's tape (stem-wrap tape)

· · ·

secateurs (pruning shears)

· · ·

dried grass heads

· · ·

raffia

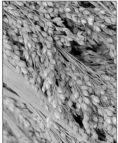

Choose the lushest grasses you can find, and don't cut off all the leaves as these lend texture to the finished piece.

The warm golden tones of this simple garland symbolize summer and harvest. Pairs of grass heads, full of seeds, are bound to a ring of garden wire with lengths of raffia. A few long, pointed leaves should be retained as they add to the texture. Many different decorative grasses are available from dried flower suppliers; if you collect your own grasses, remember that their fresh green colour will turn to gold or brown.

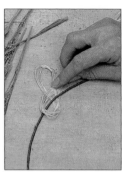

1 Using pliers, form a hook at each end of the garden wire, then bend the wire into a circle and hook the ends together. Bind the wire with florist's tape.

2 Using secateurs (pruning shears), cut each grass stem down to just below the first leaf from the top.

3 Cut a long piece of raffia and fold in half. Pass the loose ends around the wire and back through the loop to attach the raffia to the ring.

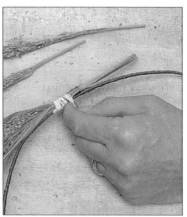

4 Take two grass heads and lay them against the outside of the ring. Using the raffia, attach them firmly to the wire by binding them at the top of the stems just under the seeds.

5 Place two more grass heads about 7.5 cm (3 in) from the first two, this time on the inside of the ring. Bind to the wire with the raffia. Repeat until the ring is covered, adding grass heads as necessary.

TEXTURED FOLIAGE RING

· · ·

MATERIALS

· · ·

scissors

· · ·

*10 stems dried natural coloured
honesty*

· · ·

*5 branches glycerine-preserved
beech leaves*

· · ·

*5 branches glycerine-preserved
adiantum*

· · ·

*60 cm (24 in) length dried
hop vine*

· · ·

*twisted wicker wreath ring,
approximately 30 cm (12 in)
diameter*

· · ·

twine

*Very easy to construct from
commercially available
materials, this foliage ring
makes a wonderful autumn
wall decoration for a hall or, if
protected from the weather, a
front door.*

Some types of foliage can be successfully air dried but many others cannot and need to be glycerine preserved.

This decoration mixes both types of foliage to create a feast of textures and subtle colours that succeeds without the enhancement of flowers.

1 Cut all the foliage stems to around 12 cm (4¾ in) long. You will need 21 lengths of each type of foliage to cover your ring. Start by securely tying a group of three stems of honesty to the wicker ring with twine.

2 Making sure it slightly overlaps the honesty, bind on a group of three glycerined beech stems with the same continuous length of twine. Repeat this process with a group of three stems of hops followed by a group of three stems of glycerined adiantum.

3 Continue binding materials to the ring in the same sequence until the ring is completely covered. Cut off any untidy stems and adjust the materials to achieve the best effect if necessary. Finally, tie off the twine in a discreet knot at the back of the ring.

GLOBE THISTLE AND MUSSEL SHELL RING

• • •

If you were wondering what to do with all those shells you collected during last year's seaside holiday, this decoration may be the answer. The material content of this display is strongly evocative of the seaside. The spiky globe thistles contrast with the smooth hard surface of the mussel shells, but probably the most memorable feature of the display is its beautiful blue colouring.

MATERIALS

· · ·

plastic foam ring for dried flowers, 13 cm (5 in) diameter

· · ·

glue gun and glue

· · ·

9 half mussel shells

· · ·

65 globe thistle heads of various sizes

· · ·

scissors

The ring would look wonderful displayed in either a bathroom or a kitchen.

1 Position groups of three slightly overlapping mussel shells at three equidistant points around the ring. Glue them to the plastic foam and to each other, taking great care when using the glue gun which will be very hot.

2 Cut the globe thistle stems to around 2.5 cm (1 in) long, put a small blob of glue on the stem and push them into the plastic foam. Continue this process until all areas of the plastic foam not covered with shells are filled.

GOLD CONE GARLAND

· · ·

Even simple materials such as rope look festive with a dusting of gold paint.

This winter garland is made from an unusual selection of materials, including larch cones, rope, chillies and small terracotta pots. Leave some of the larch branches longer than you need so that they stick out at interesting angles, and place extra material at the bottom of the garland to give it balance. It will look striking when hung on a door or window frame outside.

1 Cut off the cross-wires between the two rings and discard them. Cut the wire as close to the ring as possible or, using pliers, pull the wire away from the ring so that no sharp ends are left. Use either of the rings, depending on the size you want.

2 Tie a larch twig to the ring, using a short wire, so that the fixing is close to one end of the twig. Bend the twig gently to the shape of the ring and repeat the fixing on the other end. Repeat this all around the ring.

3 Make sure that the entire ring is covered and neatly packed. If some of the larch twigs are small or thin, add more than one at a time, crossing the ends over each other.

4 Wire each terracotta pot to the ring by passing a wire through the drainage hole and top of the pot and the ring. Twist the loose ends together and tuck the wire ends away.

5 Centre-wire three bunches of chillies (see Techniques). Attach in the same way as the pots, pushing the wire ends back into the display. Glue small pieces of moss to cover the fixings. Spray the rope gold. Tie in a bow with long ends and glue to the top of the garland. Frost the garland lightly with gold spray paint.

All the materials used here are fairly weather-resistant, so this garland will be quite happy on an exterior door.

GILDED SPICE WREATH
. . .

MATERIALS
. . .
picture framer's gilt wax
. . .
18 small dried oranges
. . .
18 short lengths of cinnamon stick, about 5 cm (2 in) long
. . .
raffia
. . .
scissors
. . .
glue gun and glue stsicks
. . .
2 large handfuls dried mace
. . .
30 cm (12 in) diameter willow wreath base
. . .
about 80 nutmegs

Gilding the oranges increases the richness of the look.

T**he** rich colours of dried oranges, cinnamon sticks and nutmeg make an unusual winter wreath with a strong aromatic scent. A layer of dried mace is used as the base for the other ingredients, which are grouped in six sections marked out by small bundles of cinnamon sticks. Rub a little gilt wax on to the oranges to bring the design to life. This lovely wreath will last indefinitely.

1 Rub a light veil of gilt wax on to the oranges.

2 Tie the cinnamon sticks into bundles of three, using raffia, and trim the ends. If you like, rub gilt wax along some of the sticks to provide highlights.

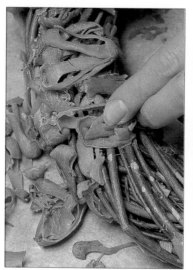

3 Using a glue gun, attach a layer of mace all over the wreath to provide a spicy base.

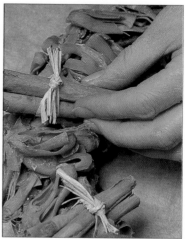

4 Add the cinnamon bundles at equal intervals to provide a framework for the rest of the design.

The finished wreath, with its glorious, rich colours and perfumed spices makes an exotic decoration.

5 Glue about three oranges in each section of the wreath, between two cinnamon bundles.

6 Add nutmegs in between the cinnamon bundles and oranges. Place more on the inside edge of the wreath, to give depth.

SHAKER-STYLE SPICE WREATH

· · ·

MATERIALS
· · ·
picture framer's gilt wax
· · ·
dried oranges
· · ·
raffia
· · ·
short cinnamon sticks
· · ·
large-eyed needle
· · ·
dried bay leaves

The two ends of raffia are simply tied to complete the wreath.

This ingenious wreath is inspired by the herbal gifts made by the Shakers, threading each item on to raffia and knotting them in place. Cinnamon sticks, dried oranges and bay leaves are threaded in repeat order to create a giant necklace of alternating colours. The result is very flexible, quite unlike wreaths made on a cane or wire base. Long swags can be made the same way, simply leaving the raffia ends untied.

1 Rub gilt wax on to the dried oranges. Wind a long strand of raffia several times around three cinnamon sticks and knot, leaving a long tail. Thread another piece of raffia underneath, on the opposite side to the knot. Adjust the two ends of raffia so they are even, then knot them securely close to the cinnamon bundle.

2 Thread both ends of raffia through a large-eyed needle. Thread on about 20 bay leaves, then an orange, then 20 more bay leaves. Remove the needle and wind the raffia strands around three more cinnamon sticks, twice in both directions. Tie the ends securely.

3 Repeat, re-threading the needle, until the length is about 85 cm (34 in). Tie the ends of raffia securely.

CINNAMON AND ORANGE RING
• • •

MATERIALS
· · ·
glue gun and glue sticks
· · ·
5 dried oranges
· · ·
plastic foam ring for dried flowers, 13 cm (5¼ in) diameter
· · ·
20 cinnamon sticks

This lovely ring would make an ideal gift – perhaps as a house-warming present, or for someone who loves cooking.

The warm colours, spicy smell and culinary content of this small decorated ring make it perfect for the wall of a kitchen.

The display is not complicated to make but requires nimble fingers to handle the very small pieces of cinnamon used. These pieces have to be tightly packed together to achieve the right effect and great care must be taken because attaching so much cinnamon to the plastic foam may cause it to collapse. To help avoid this happening you can glue the foam ring to stiff card cut to the same outline, before starting work.

1 Apply glue to the bases of the dried oranges and fix them to the plastic foam ring, equally spaced around it. Break the cinnamon sticks into 2-4 cm (¾-1½ in) pieces.

2 Apply glue to the bottom of the pieces of cinnamon and push them into the foam between the dried oranges, keeping them close together to achieve a massed effect.

3 Glue a line of the cinnamon pieces around both the inside and outside edges of the ring to cover the plastic foam completely.

FROSTED WINTER GARLAND
. . .

This design is very simple and quick to make as you can use a glue gun to attach all the materials to a ready-made base. Leave the garland in its natural state or spray it with a light coat of silver, white or gold paint for a festive effect.

MATERIALS
. . .
glue gun and glue sticks
. . .
fir cones
. . .
hop vine or twig ring
. . .
assorted nuts, e.g. brazil nuts, hazelnuts (filberts), walnuts
. . .
cinnamon sticks
. . .
wide red paper ribbon
. . .
silver, white or gold spray paint

Graduate the fir cones and nuts from a thin layer at the top of the ring to a thicker layer at the bottom.

1 Glue the fir cones to the ring in groups of 4–5, leaving a large space between each group. Attach the larger fir cones at the bottom of the ring.

2 Glue the nuts and cinnamon sticks between the fir cones, individually or in groups, again with the larger nuts at the bottom. Tie the ribbon in a large bow and glue to the top of the ring. Spray the whole design lightly with paint.

SEASHORE WREATH

. . .

MATERIALS

. . .

*70 cm (28 in) thick white
cotton rope*

. . .

masking tape

. . .

wire-cutters

. . .

garden wire

. . .

pliers

. . .

double-sided adhesive tape

. . .

white string

. . .

hand drill

. . .

*selection of shells and
dried starfish*

. . .

large-eyed needle

. . .

raffia

. . .

glue gun and glue sticks

. . .

PVA (white) glue

. . .

dried flowers, in faded colours

. . .

*wide checked or gingham
ribbon*

*Shells, starfish and other beach
souvenirs are perfect when
combined with rope.*

82

Decorate a circle of white rope with a collection of shells and starfish to
remind you of summer days by the sea. The rope base is supported by a
core of strong wire so it will keep its shape when it is hanging on a door or wall.
Place the decoration around the top of the wreath, with some of the shells
hanging down inside the circle. A large, floppy bow completes the seaside look.

1 Bind both ends of the
rope with masking tape
to prevent unravelling.
Using wire-cutters, cut a
piece of wire a little longer
than the rope. Insert
the wire into one end
of the rope.

2 Twist the rope around
the wire and push the
wire along until you reach
the other end of the rope.
The wire should now form
a core along the centre of
the rope. Bend the rope
into a circle.

3 Insert each protruding
wire into the opposite
end of the rope, so that the
wires poke through the
rope. Bend a hook at the
end of each wire, using
pliers, then push the hooks
into the core of the rope.

4 Wrap double-sided
adhesive tape around
the join, then wind white
string around it.

5 Drill holes in the tops
of the shells that you
want to hang down from
the top of the wreath.
Stitch these shells on to
the wreath using a large-
eyed needle and raffia.

6 Using buttonhole
stitch, form a raffia
loop at the back of the
wreath for hanging.
Position it in at the centre
top of your design.

7 Using a glue gun, stick more shells and starfish on to the top of the wreath, leaving the bottom part undecorated.

8 Continue to glue shells on to the inside and outside surfaces. Fill in the gaps with smaller shells, sticking them on with PVA (white) glue to avoid the risk of burning your fingers with the glue gun.

9 Stick subtly coloured dried flowers on to the wreath with PVA (white) glue, using them to fill any remaining gaps and to soften the appearance of the wreath.

10 Tie the ribbon in a bow and glue it to the centre top of the wreath. Trim the ends into 'V' shapes to prevent it from fraying.

Choose a length of ribbon that fits in with the seaside theme for the finished wreath.

SWAGS AND HANGINGS

• • •

For a stunning effect, decorate a mantelpiece or table with a gloriously rich swag, constructed on a pliable base which you can drape and loop into beautifully curved shapes. Using the same principle, make smaller hangings studded with herbs for the kitchen, or with flowers for a table display.

INTRODUCTION

· · ·

Above: Spring Flower Swag

Below: Herb Mantelpiece Border

An evergreen swag crowning a mantelpiece, a garlic and herb hanging displayed in the kitchen, or a fruit and flower swag trailing along a staircase give a truly opulent feel to your decorative schemes, and this chapter provides a wide selection to choose from.

Traditional swags made from winter foliage look wonderful displayed along the length of a fireplace, table or mantelpiece. As well as very simple winter designs such as a herb mantelpiece border made from bay leaves, rosemary and artichokes, this chapter includes really sumptuous and more challenging designs. For example, try the dried winter fireplace swag made from blue spruce, amaranthus, marjoram, holly oak, roses, lavender, chillies, oranges, green moss and gold-sprayed fir cones, embellished with a huge raffia bow and dark red ribbons.

In summer, there is always a wide choice of suitable materials to display indoors or outside. Mixed summer swags made of flowers such as larkspur, nigella and roses, with sweet-scented herbs like marjoram and oregano, are ideal for summer parties or any outdoor occasion. More unusual designs featured here include a hanging swag incorporating fabric to match your decor, and an outdoor swag studded with shells and starfish.

Swags and hangings do not have to be large and impressive to make an impact; a small decoration can make a very attractive, novel feature and is much quicker to make. The fruit window decoration is a good example and is very easy to make,

*Above: Provençal Herb
Hanging*

*Left: Lavender and
Sunflower Swag*

consisting of bundles of twigs, dried bay leaves, dried pear, apple and orange slices, fabric scraps, cinnamon sticks and gold twine. Hung in front of a window, sunlight shines through the sliced dried fruits, creating a wonderful array of natural fruity colours. If you'd like something larger but still very easy to make, the table-edge swag made from fresh conifer and dried pale pink roses is a good example – it looks lovely as a short loop along the edge of a table, and will make a very impressive addition to any table setting.

Swags and hangings, like wreaths and garlands, are built on to a base, which in this case can be a length of rope (or even string), a hay rope or a sausage of chicken wire stuffed with hay or moss. They are technically quite straightforward to create, but their sheer size often makes them a challenge. The most important thing is to have plenty of space and to lay all the materials out in a very orderly fashion. Work along the whole length of the swag or hanging to keep an even balance of materials, and so that they appear to flow together. Stand back frequently to check the design as it progresses and add delicate flowers such as roses and peonies at the end. Large swags can often be made in two or more sections, making them much easier to transport to their finished location. If you are making a single length, work from either end towards the centre; if necessary, you can disguise the point where they meet with a ribbon or raffia bow.

Below: Wheatsheaf Spiral

FLOWERPOT SWAG

· · ·

MATERIALS

· · ·

wire cutters

· · ·

chicken wire

· · ·

sphagnum moss

· · ·

.91 wires

· · ·

small terracotta pots

· · ·

scissors

· · ·

dried pink and blue larkspur

· · ·

dried blue larkspur

· · ·

dried Achillea ptarmica

· · ·

dried oregano

· · ·

dried Amaranthus caudatus

· · ·

dried yellow roses

· · ·

glue gun and glue sticks

· · ·

dried peonies

· · ·

mossing (floral) pins

· · ·

green moss

· · ·

raffia

Trailing amaranthus flowers work very well in this swag, giving it a natural country feel.

This lovely design has a chicken wire swag, filled with moss, for its base. Tiny terracotta pots are suspended along its length, blending well with the colourful selection of flowers. Add the large peony heads at the end, using them to adjust the balance of the design and also to cover any wires.

1 Make a chicken wire swag about 1.2 m (4 ft) long (see Techniques). Attach the terracotta pots by passing a wire through the drainage hole in the base and over the rim. Pass the two ends through the swag and twist them firmly together. Push the twisted ends of wire back into the swag.

2 Trim and centre-wire the larkspur, *Achillea ptarmica* and oregano. Starting with the pink larkspur, push the ends of the wires firmly into the swag base. Work the whole length of the swag, adding one variety at a time and criss-crossing the materials to create a balanced look.

3 Trim the amaranthus, leaving only 5 cm (2 in) of stem, and wire it into bunches (see Techniques). Add them along each edge of the swag, plus a few bunches along the centre between the other materials.

4 Wire small bunches of yellow roses. Put a little glue on the stems and push them into some of the terracotta pots.

5 Cut the peony heads from the stems directly under the flowers. Glue in groups of 2–3, to cover any stems or wires. Using mossing (floral) pins, attach the moss in any gaps. Tie a raffia bow and glue it to one end of the swag.

WINDOW DECORATION

· · ·

MATERIALS

· · ·

.71 florist's wires

· · ·

twigs

· · ·

picture framer's gilt wax

· · ·

dried bay leaves

· · ·

dried pear slices

· · ·

scraps of fabric

· · ·

*thick and thin dried
apple slices*

· · ·

dried orange slices

· · ·

small rubber bands

· · ·

*short lengths of
cinnamon sticks*

· · ·

gold twine

· · ·

ends of rolled beeswax candles

*Pears make a very attractive
shape when thinly sliced,
and are a good contrast to
the round oranges.*

Raid the pantry and scrap box, add garden clippings and dried fruit slices and you have all the ingredients for a delightful garland to hang in the kitchen window. The light will shine through the fruit and sparkle on the gilded twigs.

1 Wind florist's wires around the twigs to make small bundles. Rub a little gilt wax along the twigs with your finger.

2 Bend a small loop at one end of a florist's wire. Thread on some bay leaves and then a pear slice, passing the wire through the rind at top and bottom. Bend a hook at the top of the wire.

3 Tie a scrap of fabric to the bottom loop and a scrap at the top, to look like leaves. Make the apple slice bundles in the same way, threading on several thicker apple slices, followed by bay leaves.

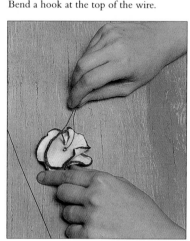

4 Wire up pairs of thinner apple slices by passing a wire through the centre. Twist the wire ends together at the top. Wire up orange slices in the same way.

This garland is designed to be hung in front of a window, where the sunlight will bring out the colours in the fruit.

5 Use small rubber bands to make up bundles of cinnamon sticks.

6 String all the elements together with gold twine. Add beeswax candle ends at intervals.

HERB MANTELPIECE BORDER
. . .

MATERIALS
. . .
wire-cutters or strong scissors
. . .
.71 florist's wires
. . .
sprigs of bay leaves
. . .
thin seagrass rope
. . .
*globe artichokes – allow 1 for
every 15 cm (6 in) of rope*
. . .
rosemary

*A simple decorative theme can
be surprisingly effective.*

The subtle colours of globe artichokes and bay leaves are celebrated in this simple design. Tie them alternately on to natural seagrass rope, then decorate the rope with rosemary. The scented herbs will give the room a lovely aroma.

1 Cut several 5 cm (2 in) lengths from the florist's wires and use them to wire the bay leaf sprigs together in bunches.

2 Cut the seagrass rope to the desired length plus an extra quarter. Tie on the artichokes at intervals, using their stalks.

3 Wire the bunches of bay leaves between the artichokes.

4 Twine the rosemary around the rope, securing it with florist's wires.

MIXED SWAG

· · ·

MATERIALS

· · ·

hay

· · ·

silver reel (rose) wire

· · ·

scissors

· · ·

*dried flowers, e.g. pink
larkspur, marjoram, nigella,
oregano, small pink roses*

· · ·

.91 wires

· · ·

raffia

· · ·

glue gun and glue sticks

*Place the flowers so that the
different varieties seem to flow
through the swag.*

This gorgeous summery swag is quite simple to make, but you do need to be careful to get the balance of materials right. If you are making a very long swag, it is easier and safer to make it in short sections and cover the joins with ribbon, otherwise you may have trouble carrying it.

2 Tie silver reel (rose) wire to one end of the hay rope. Bind on bunches of each flower variety in a zigzag fashion, winding the wire well down the stems.

1 Make a hay rope to the length required (see Techniques). Separate the flowers, ideally placing them in a semicircle within arm's reach. Trim the stems to about 18 cm (7 in).

3 Continue to the end of the rope then bind the stems together and tie a knot. Wire small bunches of a filler flower in any gaps (see Techniques). Tie and glue a large raffia bow to one end.

FLOWER AND HERB TABLE SWAG

. . .

Make a long swag by joining two shorter swags that have flowers running in opposite directions. Use the space where the swags join for a collection of candle pots, as a central focal point. The candle pots can be surrounded by some tillandsia moss and dried pomegranates, for a warm, sumptuous feeling. Include some of these materials in and around the swag, to co-ordinate the table.

MATERIALS
. . .
scissors
. . .
dried red amaranthus
. . .
dried oregano
. . .
dried red roses
. . .
dried lavender
. . .
silver reel (rose) wire
. . .
rope
. . .
.91 wires
. . .
cinnamon sticks
. . .
raffia
. . .
dried pink peonies
. . .
glue gun and glue sticks
. . .
green moss
. . .
fir cones

This arrangement benefits from the combination of materials and their vibrant mix of colour.

1 Trim all the stems of the various flowers to 15–20 cm (6–8 in). Using the silver reel (rose) wire, bind the red amaranthus and oregano in small bunches down the length of the rope, evenly spacing the bunches, with plenty of space between them.

2 Wire the roses, lavender and cinnamon sticks in small bunches (see Techniques), and decorate the cinnamon sticks with raffia bows. Push the wires through the swag, twist together and push back the sharp ends. Space the bunches evenly.

3 Cut the stems from the peony heads and glue them to the swag, spacing them evenly. Fill small gaps with moss or fir cones, gluing them in place.

95

TABLE-EDGE SWAG
· · ·

MATERIALS
· · ·
knife
· · ·
rope
· · ·
secateurs
· · ·
fresh conifer
· · ·
silver reel (rose) wire
· · ·
dried pale pink roses

The pale pink roses make this an ideal arrangement for a wedding table display.

Thís swag is very simple to make, but looks very impressive hanging in a short loop along the edge of a table for a special occasion. The fresh conifer isn't longlasting, so if you have to make it a few days before the event it is best to store it by hanging it in a cool, dry, dark place.

1 Cut the rope to the required length and make a loop at each end for hanging. Trim the conifer to short lengths and bind it to the rope, covering it all the way round, with silver reel (rose) wire.

2 Continue in the same way but adding the roses in twos and threes with a handful of conifer stems at regular intervals. Pack the conifer fairly tightly to produce a thick swag.

SUMMER TABLE SWAG
· · ·

A colourful collection of quite large materials is used to create this impressive swag, ideal for a summer evening dinner in the garden. Aim to achieve a good balance of colour and form – remember that the brighter colours, such as the pink larkspur, will stand out more than the darker colours.

MATERIALS
· · ·
scissors
· · ·
dried wheat
· · ·
dried oregano
· · ·
dried Eucalyptus spiralus
· · ·
dried pink larkspur
· · ·
dried peonies
· · ·
dried pink roses
· · ·
rope
· · ·
silver reel (rose) wire
· · ·
glue gun and glue sticks

The large ears of wheat balance well with the colours of the flowers. Use plenty of material to give a rich effect.

1 Trim all the stalks to about 15–20 cm (6–8 in) and make a pile of each variety, excluding the peonies and roses. Starting with the wheat, bind the materials to the rope in small bunches, using silver reel (rose) wire.

2 Continue to cover the rope, evenly spacing the materials along its entire length. Allow some of the material to trail on to the work surface.

3 Steam the peonies and roses (see Techniques). Cut the stems from the peony and rose heads, then glue them to the swag, spacing them evenly along the whole length.

LAVENDER AND SUNFLOWER SWAG

· · ·

MATERIALS

· · ·

plastic cases

· · ·

knife

· · ·

4 blocks plastic foam

· · ·

scissors

· · ·

10 dried sunflowers

· · ·

1 bunch dried curry flowers

· · ·

10 bunches dried lavender

Spread a little scented sunshine with vibrant sunflowers and perfumed lavender.

Giant sunflowers and scented lavender make a bold, colourful swag that gives an instant feeling of sunshine even in the depths of winter. The dried flowers will last indefinitely so the swag can be used as a permanent wardrobe decoration.

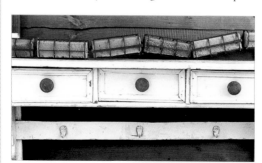

1 The swag base consists of plastic cases that link together using a hook–and–eye system.

2 Using a knife, cut the foam blocks to fit inside the cases. Link the cases together to make the desired length for the swag.

3 Cut the sunflower stems to 5 cm (2 in). Insert groups of two or three sunflowers into the foam at intervals. Add curry flowers around the sunflower groups.

4 Cut the lavender stalks to 5 cm (2 in). Insert in the foam, working outwards from the first group of sunflowers. Check that the foam is completely covered before moving on to the next group of sunflowers. Fill any spaces with curry flowers.

COUNTRY-STYLE SWAG
· · ·

· · ·

2 blocks plastic foam

· · ·

knife

· · ·

plastic cases

· · ·

secateurs (pruning shears)

· · ·

2 large bunches dill

· · ·

2 bunches bupleurum

· · ·

*2 bunches knapweed
(Centaurea montana)*

· · ·

plant spray

*Wild-looking flowers make
the prettiest table garlands for
summer meals.*

Frothy white dill and green bupleurum combine in this lovely fresh swag, with pretty purple knapweed added to give extra colour. Lay the swag along the edge of a table for a special summer occasion, adjusting the amount of materials to suit the length required.

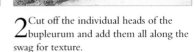

1 Thoroughly soak the foam blocks in water. Using a knife, cut them to fit inside the plastic cases. Cut the dill stems to 5 cm (2 in) and insert them into the foam to create a base.

2 Cut off the individual heads of the bupleurum and add them all along the swag for texture.

3 Finally, decorate the swag with knapweed heads for added colour. Thoroughly spray the flowers with water, using a plant spray.

HOP MANTELPIECE SWAG

· · ·

MATERIALS
· · ·

hammer

· · ·

hooks or nails

· · ·

silver reel (rose) wire

· · ·

hop bine (vine)

· · ·

*12 or more hard Conference
(Bartlett or Bosc) pears*

· · ·

picture framer's gilt wax

· · ·

.91 florist's wires

*Golden pears, with their
curvaceous lines and smooth
skins, make an excellent foil
for the delicate-looking pale
green hops.*

Pale green hop flowers and gilded pears combine beautifully in a simple swag that does not require a base. Fresh hop bines (vines) are harvested in early autumn and are pliable to work with; alternatively, you can use dried hops if you spray them with water just before using them. A single bine will reach up to 7 m (23 ft), giving a good length for a swag. This design would also look very decorative arched over a door frame.

1 Hammer hooks or nails into either side of the fireplace. Using silver reel (rose) wire attach the complete bine (vine) to the mantel shelf.

2 Using your fingers, rub each pear all over with gilt wax, allowing a little of the pear's natural tones to show through.

3 Pass florist's wire through the base of each pear and twist the ends together. Attach the pears to the hop base by winding the wires around the stems of the bine.

ARTICHOKE MANTELPIECE

SWAG

. . .

MATERIALS

. . .

string

. . .

silver reel (rose) wire

. . .

scissors

. . .

secateurs (pruning shears)

. . .

blue pine (spruce)

. . .

wire cutters

. . .

.91 wires

. . .

freeze-dried artichokes

. . .

dried pomegranates

. . .

fir cones

. . .

dried red chillies

. . .

thick rope or wide ribbon

Artichokes, pomegranates, red chillies and fir cones add extra texture and depth to the blue pine (spruce).

This grand swag is very simply created, using string and sprigs of fresh, supple blue pine (spruce) as a base for the other decorative materials. Drape it along a mantelpiece, or wind it around banisters in a hallway for an impressive welcome to your guests. The dried artichokes can be substituted if they are too hard to find.

1 Make a loop of string and attach the silver reel (rose) wire to its base, twisting it around several times to secure. Measure the string to the desired length of the swag and cut. Cut sprigs of blue pine (spruce) of roughly equal length.

2 Place a sprig of blue pine (spruce) over the loop then wind the wire around both as tightly as possible. Continue to add a few sprigs at a time along the string.

3 Alternate sides and rotate the swag to achieve a full-rounded effect. The string should be wound into the centre of the swag to act as a core and to ensure flexibility. When you reach the end, make another loop, tie with the wire and cut.

4 Wire the artichokes and pomegranates individually (see Techniques). Insert them into the body of the swag in clusters of three, starting with the artichokes and wire in position. Space each group evenly along the whole length of the swag.

5 Push the wires firmly through the body of the swag at a diagonal, then wind the prongs tightly round one another to secure. Place groups of pomegranates at regular intervals between the artichoke clusters.

String makes an unusual base for such an impressive swag, and also makes it very flexible.

6 Wire the fir cones between the natural "teeth" of the cone, as close to the base as possible. Add the fir cones in groups of three at regular intervals.

7 To prepare the chillies, take three at a time and wire the stalks together. Introduce these into the swag in large clusters between the other main groups of materials.

8 To finish, feed rope or ribbon between the various groups. Secure it to the swag at strategic points with pins made of short lengths of bent wire. Do not pull the rope or ribbon too tightly – just a little slack will look far more natural.

WINTER FIREPLACE SWAG
· · ·

MATERIALS
· · ·
knife
· · ·
thick rope
· · ·
secateurs (pruning shears)
· · ·
dried red amaranthus
· · ·
dried marjoram
· · ·
dried holly oak
· · ·
fresh blue pine (spruce)
· · ·
silver reel (rose) wire
· · ·
.91 wires
· · ·
dried red roses
· · ·
dried lavender
· · ·
dried red chillies
· · ·
dried kutchi fruit
· · ·
glue gun and glue sticks
· · ·
fir cones
· · ·
dried oranges
· · ·
green moss
· · ·
raffia

When you are working with a large number of materials it is easy to forget one or two, so check the design frequently.

106

This attractive swag is created from a rich mixture of many different materials. The blue pine (spruce) is used fresh, providing a soft base for the other dried materials. The swag will look good throughout the winter, and for Christmas you can add dark red ribbons and gold-sprayed fir cones. Remember to position the swag on the fireplace but well away from an open fire.

1 Cut the rope to the required length. Trim the amaranthus, marjoram, holly oak and blue pine (spruce) and make a pile of each. Using silver reel (rose) wire, tie small bunches to the rope, alternating the materials. Work in a zigzag fashion, leaving no spaces along the bottom, until the rope is covered.

2 Wire the roses and lavender, and centre-wire the chillies and kutchi fruit, both in small bunches. Attach these to the swag, to create a pleasing design. Glue the fir cones and oranges at intervals. Fill small gaps with moss, using glue. Tie a large raffia bow and glue to the centre of the swag.

FABRIC-DECORATED SWAG
. . .

With a design incorporating fabric, it is important to consider the final location of the display and to co-ordinate it with the decor. The terracotta pots add a rustic touch, but the design would work just as well without them. Leave the pots empty or fill them with horse chestnuts, fir cones and nuts.

MATERIALS
. . .
wire cutters
. . .
chicken wire
. . .
sphagnum moss
. . .
.91 wires
. . .
small terracotta pots
. . .
pliers
. . .
fabric
. . .
mossing (floral) pins
. . .
glue gun and glue sticks
. . .
scissors
. . .
dried lavender
. . .
dried roses
. . .
dried peonies
. . .
green moss

1 Make a chicken wire swag approximately 10 cm (4 in) in width, 2.5 cm (1 in) in depth and 60–90 cm (2–3 ft) in length (see Techniques). Attach the terracotta pots at random angles, by passing a wire through both the pot and the chicken wire. Twist the ends together with pliers.

Peonies have a striking pink colour, so try to choose a fabric that matches the flowers well.

2 Fold a strip of fabric lengthways into three to make a band about 10 cm (4 in) wide. Scrunch up one end and pin it to the top of the swag, using a mossing (floral) pin. Wrap the fabric down the length of the swag and around the pots, letting it hang fairly loosely. Every 15 cm (6 in), fix it with another pin. Make sure the raw edges are at the back. Pull the fabric into shape, scrunch up the other end, tuck it under the last pot and pin.

3 Make a fabric bow (see Techniques). Glue it to the top of the swag, using a glue gun. Trim the lavender and roses to 15 cm (6 in) then centre-wire them in bunches. Push the wires into the swag, with a little of the flowers covering the fabric. Criss-cross the bunches at random until the frame and moss are covered. Cut the peony heads from their stems and glue down the length of the swag. Fill any spaces with moss.

SEASIDE SWAG

· · ·

MATERIALS

· · ·

wire cutters

· · ·

chicken wire

· · ·

sphagnum moss

· · ·

.91 wires

· · ·

small terracotta pots

· · ·

dried Eryngium alpinum

· · ·

glue gun and glue sticks

· · ·

dried echinops

· · ·

dried Eucalyptus spiralus

· · ·

shells

· · ·

starfish

· · ·

mossing (floral) pins

· · ·

reindeer moss

· · ·

dried yellow roses

· · ·

raffia

The materials used in this swag make it ideal for damp conditions.

This large swag is made from a wide collection of materials, combining dried flowers and leaves with seashells, starfish and small flowerpots. It makes an exuberant summer decoration to display outdoors.

1 Make a chicken wire swag about 1.2 m (4 ft) long (see Techniques). Fix several pots along its length, by passing a wire through the drainage hole in the base and over the rim. Pass the ends of the wire through the swag, then twist firmly together and push back into the swag.

2 Centre-wire the eryngium. Push the ends of the wire firmly into the swag. Work gradually along the whole length, criss-crossing the bunches of eryngium.

3 Glue small bunches of echinops on to the swag. Space them along the whole length of the swag, covering both the sides and the top. Wire the eucalyptus (see Techniques) and place in bunches along the swag and around the pots.

4 Attach the shells and starfish, making sure that the glue comes into contact with the chicken wire frame, the stems and the wires.

5 Using mossing (floral) pins, fix reindeer moss into any gaps. Finally, bunch the roses and push 4–5 into some of the pots. Tie the raffia into a large bow and glue it to one end of the swag.

STARFISH SWAG

· · ·

MATERIALS

· · ·

scissors

· · ·

rope

· · ·

glue gun and glue sticks

· · ·

starfish

· · ·

tillandsia moss

· · ·

dried eucalyptus

· · ·

.91 wires

· · ·

shells

· · ·

lichen moss

· · ·

small branches

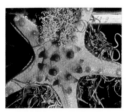

The distinctive shapes of starfish make this swag very appealing.

This small swag is full of character, with an unusual and interesting mix of materials. It can be viewed from both sides, making it ideal for placing against a window or mirror. The starfish swag would be ideal for a bathroom, where dried flowers and herbs are less suitable.

1 Cut a length of rope 1–1.2 m (3–4 ft) long. Randomly tie knots along its length and make a loop at one end.

2 Place a blob of glue on one side of a starfish and lay the rope across it, between two knots.

3 Glue a second starfish over the top of the first, trapping the rope between the two. Tuck some tillandsia moss around the edges of the two starfish, so that some of it hangs out of the sides. Repeat at several points along the rope.

4 Trim the eucalyptus to 20 cm (8 in) lengths. Using wires, fix several pieces to the rope in one place. Repeat along the rope about every 25 cm (10 in).

5 Glue a shell at the base of the eucalyptus bunches. Work around the rope until the bases of the stems and the wires are covered. Attach a little lichen moss and add occasional pieces of branch. Repeat along the whole length of the rope at varying intervals.

FRUIT AND FLOWER SWAG

. . .

MATERIALS

. . .

.71 wires

. . .

4 limes

. . .

9 lemons

. . .

4 bunches black grapes

. . .

4 bunches sneezeweed
(Helenium)

. . .

1 bundle tree ivy

. . .

scissors

. . .

straw plait (braid), about
60 cm (24 in) long

. . .

raffia

. . .

1 bunch ivy trails (sprigs)

The component parts have to
be wired, but otherwise the
swag is simple to construct. Do
remember that although lemons
and limes will survive in this
situation, grapes and cut
flowers will need regular mist
spraying with water.

T he colour and content of this decorative swag will brighten any room. Its visual freshness makes it especially suitable for a kitchen but, if it was made on a longer base, the decoration could be a mantelpiece garland or even extended to adorn the balustrade of a staircase.

1 First, all the fruit has to be wired. Pass a wire through from side to side just above the base of the limes. Leave equal lengths of wire projecting from either side, bend these down and twist together under the base. If the lemons are heavier than the limes, pass a second wire through at right angles to the first, providing four equal ends to be twisted together under their bases.

2 Group the grapes in small clusters and double leg mount with .71 wires. Then form 12 small bunches of sneezeweed mixed with tree ivy and double leg mount these on .71 wires.

3 Starting at its bottom end, bind three wired lemons to the plait (braid) with raffia. Then in turn bind a bunch of flowers and foliage, a lime, grapes and a second bunch of flowers and foliage.

4 Repeat binding materials to the plait in the above sequence until almost at the top. Secure by wrapping the remaining raffia tightly around the plait.

5 Make a bow from raffia and tie to the top of the swag. Trim off any stray wire ends. Entwine the ivy trails (sprigs) around the top of the swag and bow.

SPRING FLOWER SWAG

· · ·

MATERIALS

· · ·

*secateurs (pruning shears) or
wire-cutters*

· · ·

chicken wire

· · ·

scissors

· · ·

black plastic rubbish (trash) bag

· · ·

*2 pansy plants per 15 cm
(6 in) of swag*

· · ·

*6 viola plants per 15 cm (6 in)
of swag*

· · ·

.71 florist's wires

· · ·

moss

*Pretty little pansies and violas
add a wonderful, woodland feel
to this springtime swag.*

Transplant small pansy and viola plants into a swag base so that they will continue to grow. The plants are placed in individual bags of black plastic to prevent any soil or water escaping, and a covering of moss gives a very natural effect. Any small nursery plants could be used, to complement your table setting.

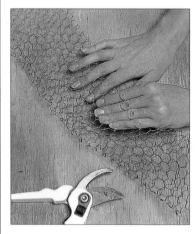

1 Cut the chicken wire to the desired length of the swag and three times the width. Form it into a flattened roll.

2 Cut the black plastic bag into squares large enough to cover the rootballs of the pansies and violas.

3 One by one, unpot each plant, gently remove any loose soil and place the rootball in the centre of a black plastic square.

4 Gather the plastic around the rootball. Secure it in place by winding a wire loosely around the top, leaving a short length free to fix to the swag.

5 Attach the bagged-up plants to the swag, using the free ends of wire.

6 Cover any visible plastic with moss, fixing it with short lengths of florist's wire bent into U-shaped pins.

PROVENÇAL HERB HANGING
. . .

MATERIALS
. . .

scissors

. . .

seagrass string

. . .

garden twine

. . .

silver reel (rose) wire

. . .

sage

. . .

thyme

. . .

oregano

. . .

2 small terracotta flowerpots

. . .

.91 florist's wires

. . .

2 garlic heads

. . .

glue gun and glue sticks (optional)

. . .

large dried red chillies

Garlic gives this hanging a spicy, Provençal flavour.

Make the most of fresh, aromatic summer herbs by hanging them on a braided rope of seagrass, a perfect gift from a gardener for anyone who loves to cook. Tiny terracotta flowerpots are wired on to the braid, filled with large red chillies which contrast with the soft green colours of the herbs and the fat white bulbs of garlic.

1 Cut six lengths of seagrass string about three times as long as the desired finished length of the hanging. Take two lengths, fold them in half and place them under a length of garden twine. Pass the cut ends over the twine and through the loop of the fold, thereby knotting the seagrass on to the garden twine. Repeat twice with the remaining four seagrass lengths. Divide the seagrass into three bundles of four lengths and braid them together.

2 Finish the end of the braid by binding it with a separate piece of seagrass string.

3 Using silver reel (rose) wire, bind the herbs into small bundles. Tie each bundle with garden twine to cover the wire. Using the twine, tie them to the braided base.

4 Wire the flowerpots by passing two wires through the central hole and twisting the ends together.

5 Wire the pots to the braid by passing a wire through the wires on the pots, passing it through the braid, then twisting the ends together.

6 Tie twine around the garlic heads, then tie these to the braid. Wire or glue the chillies in position, and fill the pots with more chillies.

WHEATSHEAF SPIRAL

• • •

MATERIALS

· · ·

sheaves of wheat

· · ·

ball of string

· · ·

scissors

· · ·

wire-cutters

· · ·

heavy-gauge garden wire

· · ·

thick rope

Prepare plenty of bunches of wheat in advance to speed up the assembly time.

The natural colours of golden wheat and thick rope combine in this impressive hanging. Small bunches of wheat are laid diagonally on top of each other to create the spiral pattern, which is then accentuated by the coils of rope. Prepare plenty of bunches of wheat before you start so that you can build up a good rhythm as you work. The hanging should last for years.

1 Strip the wheat stems and put them into small bunches. Wind string around the stems, close to the heads. Tie in a secure knot and trim the ends.

2 Trim the stems, leaving approximately 10 cm (4 in). Make up several small bunches.

3 Attach the ball of string to the first bunch, then place the second bunch diagonally across the first. Wrap the string several times around both bunches.

4 Add more bunches until you have achieved the required length, tie a knot with the string and cut. Wire the thick rope to the top as deep into the spiral as possible to conceal the wire.

5 Gently wind the rope through the spiral gaps as neatly as possible. The rope should fit snugly into the crevices to camouflage the string ties.

6 When you reach the bottom, make a large loop out of the rope. Tie the string several times around the wheat and the rope to hold it in position.

7 Wind the excess rope neatly around the wheat ends in a spiral, pulling it as tightly as possible to avoid movement.

8 Cut a length of heavy-gauge wire. Secure the end of the rope by threading the wire through the body of the garland and twisting it back and around itself.

DRIED GRASS HARVEST SWAG

· · ·

MATERIALS

· · ·

*1 bunch dried, natural
triticale*

· · ·

*1 bunch dried, natural
linseed*

· · ·

*1 bunch dried, natural
Nigella orientalis*

· · ·

*1 bunch dried, natural
phalaris*

· · ·

scissors

· · ·

.71 wires

· · ·

*1 straw plait, approximately
60 cm (24 in) long*

· · ·

twine

· · ·

raffia

*Although a good deal of
wiring is required for the
construction of this swag, it is
relatively straightforward and
enjoyable to make.*

T his harvest swag is a symbolic collection of dried decorative grasses. It relies on the subtlety of colour differences and textural variation in the grasses for its natural, yet splendid, effect.

In a church at harvest time the swag could be hung on a wall, or a series of them could be mounted on the ends of the pews. In the home it could be hung on a wall, or extended to decorate a mantelpiece.

1 Split each bunch of grass into 8 smaller bunches, giving you 32 individual bunches. Cut the stems to approximately 15 cm (6 in) long and double leg mount the individual groups with .71 wires.

2 Start by tying a wired bunch of triticale to the bottom of the plait with the twine. Then place a bunch of linseed above, to the left and slightly overlapping the triticale, and bind this on to the plait with the twine. Follow this with a bunch of *Nigella orientalis* above, to the right, and slightly overlapping the triticale. Finish the sequence by positioning a bunch of phalaris directly above the triticale, slightly overlapping, and bind on with the twine.

3 Repeat this pattern eight times to use all four varieties of grasses, binding each bunch on to the plait with the twine.

4 When all the grasses have been used and the top of the plait reached, tie off with the twine and trim any excess wires.

5 Make a bow from the raffia and tie it on to the top of the decorated plait, covering the wires and the twine.

RINGS AND
CIRCLETS

• • •

*For a special day, decorate your table with pretty
flower-filled circlets, basket edgings, napkin
rings and candle holders. Many of these
designs are quite quick to make and are sure
to enchant your guests.*

INTRODUCTION
· · ·

*Above: Lavender Candlestick
Circlets*

Below: Hydrangea Ring

Flower-filled rings and circlets make perfect decorations for the table: they won't obstruct the diners' view of each other, they can't be knocked over and they are always a conversation-piece.

Table decorations such as a white lilac ring or a chamomile ring are very easy to make, and look extremely effective when used to decorate a special fruit dessert. Making a circlet for a bowl is very similar to making a wreath or garland: select a florist's foam ring in the size required, soak it in water and add stems of fresh or dried flowers. The design can be as simple or as extravagant as you like – embellish your arrangements with seasonal herbs and green foliage to create a delicious, lush effect. If you are using fresh flowers, keep the circlet fresh by spraying it with water before placing a bowl or plate in the middle.

Another idea is to make your own basket edgings, for example, using fruit or hydrangeas. This is a great way to give an old wicker basket a new lease of life, and if you use dried flowers the basket should last a long time. Napkin rings, too, make lovely table decorations and are easily constructed using a wire or raffia base. Several of the table centrepieces included here are designed to be taken apart and reassembled on another occasion, each time adding to or adjusting the arrangement to keep it interesting.

Above: Floating Candle Ring

Left: Chamomile Ring

The second half of the chapter consists of projects involving the use of candles. These include tiny rings surrounding candles, small candlestick circlets and candle pots bordered with flowers, as well as larger projects such as a hydrangea candle ring, which supports four candles. The small candle decoration ideas shown here are very quick and simple to make, often requiring no wiring or technical skills and very few materials. They can be made very inexpensively from individual flowers and materials left over from larger projects, and are easily adaptable to suit the occasion.

A very effective way to mix candles and flowers is in a chandelier. These are quite easy to make, using a garland ring as a base and decorating it with summer flowers or gilded fruits according to the season. They never fail to enchant with their fragile, magical candlelight.

The success of these designs rests on getting the right balance between the candle and the base. Always position candles very carefully, and remember that longer candles are more vulnerable to accidents than short, fat candles in pots. If you are dining by candlelight, sit the candles in the centre or attach small pots to a ring before adding flowers so that you can tuck the candles in afterwards. For winter decorations, use aromatic spices and fruit with fresh or dried foliage. Stunning effects can be created by contrasting the formality of a ring with arrangements that spill out in all directions. When using your new candle decorations, remember never to leave them unattended when burning.

Below: Hop Flower Candle Ring

WHITE LILAC RING

· · ·

MATERIALS

· · ·

*20 cm (8 in) diameter plastic
foam ring*

· · ·

secateurs (pruning shears)

· · ·

about 30 heads of white lilac

· · ·

viburnum leaves

*Sharp green, white and blue
always look fresh in spring.*

For a special occasion, decorate the table with a simple ring of sweet-smelling lilac, then surprise your guests by placing the dessert in the centre. Add a few green leaves, such as viburnum, to the ring to contrast with the frothy white lilac flowers. Choose a glass bowl for the dessert to create an enchanting centrepiece.

1 Thoroughly soak the foam ring and leave to drain. Cut the lilac stems to within about 2.5 cm (1 in) of the flowers and push into the ring.

2 Position the larger flowers so they drape towards the outside of the ring. Use smaller heads to cover the inside edge of the ring.

3 Add viburnum leaves, spacing them evenly around the ring.

CHAMOMILE RING

· · ·

MATERIALS

· · ·

20 cm (8 in) diameter plastic foam ring

· · ·

bowl, to fit inside the ring

· · ·

1 large bunch oregano

· · ·

2 large bunches rosemary

· · ·

1 large bunch chamomile flowers

Spare chamomile flowers placed in a glass of water make a delightful table arrangement.

For summer entertaining, surround a small bowl of fruit with a ring of aromatic oregano and rosemary leaves, then add the tiny white daisy-like flowers of the chamomile plant. Rich red strawberries look perfect within the fresh green and white border. Once cut, keep the herbs in water until you are ready to use them.

1 Soak the foam ring in water and place on the work surface with the bowl in the centre.

2 Push in oregano stems around the edge and top of the ring to make a base.

3 Fill out the rest of the ring with rosemary, making sure that no foam shows and that the bowl is hidden. Finally, add the chamomile flowers.

128

FENNEL-DECORATED RING

· · ·

MATERIALS

· · ·

20 cm (8 in) diameter plastic
foam ring

· · ·

scissors

· · ·

large bunch mint

· · ·

large bunch flat leaf parsley

· · ·

2 fennel flowerheads

· · ·

knife

· · ·

plate, to fit inside the ring

· · ·

plant spray

*You will need quite a lot of
material to fill the ring, so the
trick is to choose seasonal
herbs, which will be abundant
and give a lush, deliciously
aromatic finished effect.*

Florets of fennel add an extra texture to this attractive herbal ring, their aniseed scent mingling with the aromatic mint in the base. Make the ring in summer when the herbs are in season and are looking their best. The green leaves act as a perfect foil for serving colourful berry fruits.

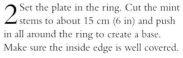

1 Soak the foam ring in water until it is wet through. Snip off the ends of the herb stems and plunge them into water until you are ready. Shave off the inner edge of the foam ring with a knife to give a softer shape.

2 Set the plate in the ring. Cut the mint stems to about 15 cm (6 in) and push in all around the ring to create a base. Make sure the inside edge is well covered.

3 Prepare the parsley in the same way as the mint. Use to fill in any space, and to generously fill the lower edge, making a 'skirt' to cover the plastic base of the ring completely.

4 Cut off the fennel
florets and add. Spray
the ring well with water.

*Mint, flat leaf parsley
and fennel flowers make a
sophisticated green frame
for the fruit.*

HYDRANGEA RING

· · ·

MATERIALS

· · ·

40 cm (16 in) diameter plastic foam ring

· · ·

green plate, to fit inside the ring

· · ·

secateurs (pruning shears)

· · ·

10 hydrangea heads and leaves

Purple and green may seem an unlikely colour combination, but here it is arresting.

In early autumn the large, showy heads of hydrangeas fade to subtle shades of old rose, which are a lovely accompaniment to autumn fruits such as figs and plums. The flowers are bold enough to use on their own, with just a few of their own leaves creating a very natural effect.

1 Soak the foam ring in water, then place the plate in the middle. Cut the hydrangea stems to about 2.5 cm (1 in).

2 Insert the hydrangea stems into the foam to cover it completely. Add a few leaves.

HYDRANGEA BASKET EDGING

· · ·

Hydrangea heads cut late in their growing season have toughened and will not wilt out of water. These together with autumn leaves, selected so that they are pliable enough to wire, have been used in a floral decoration which can evolve from fresh to dry and remain attractive.

Take mature hydrangea heads and some autumn leaves, and with a little imagination an old wicker basket is transformed into a delightful container. Whether you fill it with fruit or seasonal pot pourri, this basket will make a decorative and long-lasting addition to your home.

1 Wire the leaves by stitching and double leg mounting on .71 wires.

2 Wire clusters of hydrangea by double leg mounting on .71 wires.

3 Secure the wired hydrangea clusters and leaves alternately around the basket edge by stitching through the gaps in the basket with .32 silver reel (rose) wire. Keep the clusters tightly together to ensure a full edging.

4 When the entire basket edge is covered, finish by stitching the .32 reel wire through several times. If the arrangement is placed in an airy position, the hydrangea heads will dry naturally and prolong the basket's use.

FRUIT AND FUNGI BASKET
RIM DECORATION
• • •

MATERIALS

• • •

45 slices dried orange

• • •

45 slices dried lemon

• • •

*45 slices preserved
(dried) apple*

• • •

.71 wires

• • •

18 sunflower heads

• • •

16 small pieces dried fungus

• • •

florist's tape (stem-wrap tape)

• • •

scissors

• • •

*old wicker basket, without
a handle*

• • •

.32 silver reel (rose) wire

*The principles of this design
can be used to decorate a
wicker container of any type.*

Creating a dried flower embellishment for the rim of an old and damaged wicker basket gives it a new lease of life by transforming it into a resplendent container for the display of fruit. The decoration is full of the bold textures and rich colours of sunflowers, oranges, lemons, apples and fungi.

1 Group the orange slices in threes and double leg mount each group with .71 wires. Repeat with the lemon and apple slices. Cut the sunflower stems to about 2.5 cm (1 in) and individually double leg mount them on .71 wires. Double leg mount the pieces of fungi with .71 wire. Finally tape over all the wires with florist's tape (stem-wrap tape).

2 Starting at one corner of the basket, bind a group of orange slices to its rim by stitching .32 silver reel (rose) wire through the wicker and around the stem. With the same wire, stitch on the apple slices, the sunflower heads, the lemon slices and the fungi. Repeat this sequence until the rim is covered. Twist the wire around the last stem and the basket.

HERBAL TABLE DECORATION
. . .

This table decoration is made up of five elements: four terracotta pots of various herbs, foliages contained within a plastic foam ring, night–lights (tea–lights) and white dill. This is an interesting alternative to the more conventional concept of an arrangement held in plastic foam, or wire mesh, in a single container.

MATERIALS
. . .
6 night–lights (tea–lights)
. . .
30 cm (12 in) diameter plastic
foam wreath frame
. . .
2 blocks plastic foam
. . .
4 terracotta pots
. . .
cellophane (plastic wrap)
. . .
scissors
. . .
white dill
. . .
rosemary
. . .
mint
. . .
marjoram
. . .
guelder rose
(Viburnum opulus)
(European cranberry) berries

This display can be dismantled and the parts used separately to good effect in different situations. The individual terracotta pots of herbs can even be dried and their usefulness extended. Never leave burning candles unattended.

1 Press the night–lights (tea–lights) into the soaked plastic foam ring, at equal distances around its circumference. Soak the block of plastic foam and line the terracotta pots with cellophane to prevent leakage. Cut the plastic foam to size and fit it firmly into the pots.

2 Mass the white dill around the base ring between the night–lights (tea–lights). Then mass the individual pots with selected herbs and foliage. The effect is greater if each pot is filled with one type of herb only. Position the base ring and arrange the pots within it.

DAISY AND HERB
NAPKIN RINGS
· · ·

MATERIALS
· · ·
FOR THE DAISY RING
wire-cutters
· · ·
garden wire
· · ·
florist's tape (stem-wrap tape)
· · ·
daisies
· · ·
scissors
· · ·
plant spray
· · ·
FOR THE HERB RING
scissors
· · ·
fennel flowerhead
· · ·
green raffia
· · ·
lavender
· · ·
plant spray

What could be more charming than simple napkin rings made from fresh meadow flowers and herbs?

These enchanting little rings are made by two different techniques. The daisy ring has a wire base, on to which the flowers are bound with florist's tape (stem-wrap tape). The herb ring is simply fennel and lavender flowers bound alternately on to green raffia. Make these delightful napkin rings at the last minute and spray them well to keep them fresh.

1 To make the daisy ring, cut a piece of garden wire long enough to encircle the napkin. Bind the end with florist's tape (stem-wrap tape).

2 Wrap the tape around the wire, binding in flowers as you go to cover the piece of wire completely. Bend the wire into a ring and tape the ends together. Spray well with water.

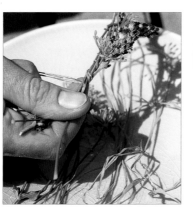

3 To make the herb ring, cut the florets off the fennel flowerhead. Using green raffia and leaving a short length free at the beginning, bind alternate lavender and fennel florets into a small circlet.

4 When the circlet is the right length, spray it well with water. Place it around the rolled napkin and tie the ends of the raffia neatly together.

EUCALYPTUS AND HELLEBORE CANDLE RING

. . .

MATERIALS

. . .

knife

. . .

18 cm (7 in) diameter plastic foam ball

. . .

23 cm (9 in) diameter plate

. . .

4 church candles, each 2.5 cm (1 in) diameter

. . .

scissors

. . .

1 bunch small-leaved eucalyptus

. . .

16 white hellebore flowers

The purity of this candle ring perfectly complements classic church candles.

Blue-green eucalyptus leaves and beautiful white hellebore flowers make a very elegant winter decoration. The waxy petals of the hellebore flowers echo the creamy white church candles; if hellebores are not in season, white anemones make a good substitute. Extinguish the candles before they reach the level of the leaves and flowers.

1 Cut the foam ball in half to fit on the plate. Soak the foam in water and allow to drain. Using a knife, cut the bottom ends off three of the candles to create varying lengths. Push the candles into the centre of the foam.

2 Cut the eucalyptus into pieces about 15 cm (6 in) long. Insert them into the foam to cover it.

3 Cut the hellebore flower stems to about 13 cm (5 in) long and add at random to the arrangement.

PARROT TULIP CANDLE DECORATION

· · ·

MATERIALS

· · ·

plastic foam ring, 15 cm (6 in)
diameter, and holder

· · ·

candle, 7.5 x 22.5 cm
(3 x 9 in)

· · ·

scissors

· · ·

approximately 7-8 very open
'Parrot' tulip heads

Other flowers, such as roses and buttercups can, when their flowerheads are full, have their useful lives extended by the use of this technique.
Never leave a burning candle unattended and do not allow it to burn down to within less than 5 cm (2 in) of the display height.

There is a tendency to think that a fully opened bloom is at the end of its useful life. However, these Parrot tulip heads have had their lives extended by the simple process of shortening their stems. The red and yellow of the spreading petals of these tulips create an impression of flames licking up the candle.

1 Soak the plastic foam ring in water and position the candle at its centre. Check that the candle is firmly in position.

2 Cut the tulips to a stem length of approximately 3 cm (1¼ in) and push them into the plastic foam. Repeat this around the entire ring making sure no foam is left exposed.

BERRIED CANDLE DECORATION

· · ·

A commercially-produced red candle in an earthenware pot can be made into a sumptuous table decoration by embellishing it with fruits and foliage from the garden and hedge. This is a technically simple, yet effective, decoration involving sitting the pot in a small wire basket through which the stems of fruit and foliage are artfully woven.

MATERIALS

· · ·

candle in an earthenware pot

· · ·

small square wire basket, to accommodate the pot

· · ·

Virginia creeper leaves on stems

· · ·

blackberry clusters on stems

· · ·

scissors

· · ·

rosehip clusters on stems

· · ·

.32 silver reel (rose) wire

1 Place the candle pot in the wire basket. Weave Virginia creeper stems through the wire basket around its entire top edge. Then establish a thick garland of Virginia creeper leaves around the basket.

2 For safe handling strip the thorns from the blackberry stems and cut to approximately 6 cm (2 in) long. Push the stems into the Virginia creeper garland and through the wire basket.

The plant materials used are robust enough to survive in good condition for a day or two out of water but would benefit from mist spraying. Never leave burning candles unattended and do not allow them to burn down to within 5 cm (2 in) of the display.

3 Using the same procedure, add the rosehips but in separate small groups around the circumference of the basket. If the decoration is likely to be moved, it is safer to provide additional security for the stems by tying them to the basket with lengths of fine silver reel (rose) wire.

FRESH ROSE CANDLE RING

. . .

MATERIALS

. . .

plastic foam ball

. . .

knife

. . .

glass bowl

. . .

candle

. . .

secateurs (pruning shears)

. . .

open garden roses, including leaves and rosehips

Pick full-blown roses from the garden – the delicate yellow stamens in the centres add extra appeal.

Full-blown roses have a lovely informal character, quite different to tightly furled roses. Use a mixture of different varieties, depending on what is available, and place them in a decorative glass bowl. The warmth of the candle will release the scent from the roses – remember to extinguish the candle before it reaches the level of the display.

1 Thoroughly soak the foam ball in water for at least half an hour. Cut the ball in half.

2 Place one of the soaked halves in the glass bowl and push the candle into the middle.

3 Trim the rose stems to about 2.5 cm (1 in). Insert the roses to cover the foam base completely.

4 Add a few leaves and rosehips to complete the candle ring and give it a wilder, less contrived appearance.

CABBAGE CANDLE RING

· · ·

MATERIALS

· · ·

knife

· · ·

1 block plastic foam

· · ·

5 cm (2 in) diameter candle

· · ·

plate

· · ·

ornamental cabbage

Purple veins make a stunning tracery pattern in blue-green cabbage leaves.

Amuse your guests with this witty candle ring, made from the colourful leaves of an ornamental cabbage plant. Many different varieties and colours are now available. The candle ring is very quick to make, using just a few large leaves. Soak the foam thoroughly first so that the leaves will not wilt too quickly.

1 Cut a square from the florist's foam large enough to fix the candle in, leaving a margin of about 1 cm (½ in) all round. Thoroughly soak the foam in water and leave to drain. Place it in the middle of the plate, then push the candle into the centre.

2 Trim away the top edge of the foam all around the candle. Break the leaves off the cabbage and, working from the bottom, push them face up into the sides of the foam.

3 For the top layer, place the underside of the leaves uppermost so that they fan away from the candle.

FLOATING CANDLE RING
. . .

MATERIALS
. . .
plastic foam ring with integral
plastic tray
. . .
jug
. . .
flower food
. . .
scissors
. . .
purple statice
. . .
pointed stick or skewer
. . .
.91 florist's wires
. . .
tindori
. . .
wire-cutters
. . .
yellow habanero chillies
. . .
bi-coloured carnations
. . .
gerbera flowers
. . .
small zinnia flowers
. . .
shallow glass dish, to fit
inside the ring
. . .
glass pebbles
. . .
floating candles

*Statice bought fresh will dry
very successfully.*

Vividly coloured flowers mixed with tiny exotic vegetables give this ring an exuberant character, ideal for a party buffet table. The ornamental carnations stand out against the display of different materials, which are reflected in a candlelit pool of water. Make the candle ring to fit your table space, choosing a foam ring the appropriate size. The floating candles will burn down safely inside the bowl of water.

1 Soak the foam ring thoroughly, using water with flower food added. Cut off the statice flowers, leaving about 5 cm (2 in) of stem. Use a pointed stick or skewer to make a hole in the foam before inserting each stem. Add the statice flowers to the top and sides of the foam, leaving spaces for the other materials.

2 Push a wire through the base of each tindori. Trim the wire to leave about 5 cm (2 in) sticking out from each side. Gently pull the ends down and twist together to make a rigid 'stalk'.

3 Push a wire through the base or side of each chilli, then cut and twist it as for the tindori. (Wash your hands after handling chillies as the juice can be very painful if rubbed near your eyes.)

4 Cut the carnation stems to about 2.5 cm (1 in). Make a hole in the foam with the stick or skewer before gently pressing in each stem.

5 Arrange the gerbera flowers in the same way, handling them very gently as they are not as robust as the carnations and may snap.

6 Any remaining spaces may be filled
with small zinnia flowers, cutting the
stems short as for the carnations and gerbera.

7 Fill a shallow glass dish with glass
pebbles and floating candles. Arrange
it within the wreath on the table and fill it
carefully with water.

*This shallow dish of floating
candles adorned with brightly
coloured flowers and tiny
vegetables would make a pretty
centrepiece for a buffet table.*

LAVENDER CANDLESTICK CIRCLETS

· · ·

MATERIALS

· · ·

wire-cutters

· · ·

garden wire

· · ·

scissors

· · ·

dried lavender

· · ·

silver reel (rose) wire

· · ·

narrow satin ribbon

As well as being beautiful decorations, these candlestick circlets will add to the ambience of your table with their relaxing aroma.

These pretty little decorations are very popular in Scandinavia, using many different materials. Here, sweet-scented dried lavender makes a very simple circlet that can be used again and again. Vary the colour of the ribbon, if you wish, to match the colour of different candles. Extinguish the candles before they burn down to the level of the flowers.

1 Make a ring of garden wire that will slip easily over the candle but sit snugly on top of the candlestick. Wind the wire ends around the ring to secure them. Trim the lavender stems to about 1 cm (½ in). Using silver reel (rose) wire, bind a few stems at a time to make small bunches.

2 Bind the bunches of lavender to the wire ring with silver reel (rose) wire. Thread ribbon through the ring and tie in a bow.

DRIED ROSE CANDLE RINGS

. . .

Any small-headed flowers would be suitable for these attractive decorations but dried miniature roses are perfect. If you are using more than one shade of rose on a candle ring, glue them in pairs of different colours and position the heads so that they are facing outwards. Small leaves discarded with the unwanted rose stems make useful fillers, but take care that they are not too tall and may become a fire hazard. Never leave lighted candles unattended.

MATERIALS

. . .

glue gun and glue sticks

. . .

moss

. . .

small cane ring

. . .

scissors

. . .

dried flowers, e.g. miniature roses, bupleurum

. . .

candle

. . .

moss

Make the candle ring any size, depending on the width of your candle.

1 Glue a light covering of moss to the cane ring. Try to make sure that no glue is visible.

2 Trim the rose heads from their stems, leaving as little stalk as possible. Glue them in place in a balanced and symmetrical design.

3 Fill the spaces between the roses with other flowers or foliage, leaving enough room for the candle. Fill any remaining gaps with moss.

CANDLE CUFF
· · ·

MATERIALS
· · ·
candle
· · ·
plain white paper
· · ·
scissors
· · ·
thick brown paper
· · ·
clear tape (cellophane)
· · ·
hessian (burlap)
· · ·
glue gun and glue sticks
· · ·
rope
· · ·
.91 wire
· · ·
twigs
· · ·
green moss
· · ·
dried miniature roses

The combination of dark and pale pink roses is exquisite.

Choose a wide candle so that the cuff is large enough to apply the dried flower materials. The candle must be at least twice the height of the cuff, so that it has plenty of room to burn without any danger of setting the hessian (burlap) alight. Wrap the candle well at the start of the project to ensure that it is kept clean and that the hot glue does not melt the wax.

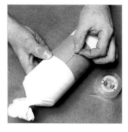

1 Wrap the candle in plain paper. Cut a piece of brown paper approximately 8 cm (3 in) wide and long enough to wrap around the candle. Tape the loose end down; the paper collar must be able to move freely up and down the candle.

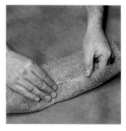

2 Cut a piece of hessian (burlap) twice as wide as the brown paper and long enough to wrap round the candle. Fold the two outer quarters up to meet in the middle and glue them down.

3 Lay the candle on the wrong side of the hessian (burlap) and apply a little glue to either side of the candle. Wrap the hessian (burlap) tightly around the candle, smoothing it to fit the paper neatly, and applying glue where necessary.

4 Trim the corners of the exposed edge of hessian (burlap) and glue them down sparingly.

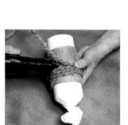

5 Wrap the rope around the hessian (burlap) cuff once and hold it in place. Apply glue all the way around the rope, so that the glue comes into contact with both the rope and the hessian (burlap). Wrap the rope around the candle again, as close as possible to the first wrap. Repeat until the whole cuff is covered.

6 Centre-wire a small bundle of twigs. Glue the bundle and some green moss to the cuff at an angle, using the moss to cover the wire. Cut the heads from the roses and glue them in place around the bundle of twigs.

ROSE-PERFUMED CANDLE POTS

. . .

MATERIALS

. . .

hay

. . .

silver reel (rose) wire, string or raffia

. . .

scissors

. . .

terracotta pot

. . .

glue gun and glue sticks

. . .

moss

. . .

dried roses

. . .

small-leaved green foliage

. . .

rose-perfumed oil

. . .

candle

Small roses can be inserted into any gaps in the design left by larger rose heads.

These two candle pots are variations of the same theme. One is a very simple combination of roses and foliage, while the other combines large as well as miniature roses, while using a larger candle. You could make a selection of small displays for dinner parties, using the larger pot as a centrepiece with vibrant green moss and small fruits arranged around the base. The wonderful long-lasting scent of the rose oil will be accentuated by the heat of the candle. Remember never to leave lighted candles unattended.

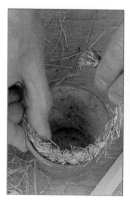
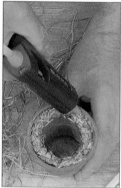

1 Make a small hay collar to fit inside the rim of the pot (see Techniques).

2 Glue the collar inside the rim of the pot, as close to the top as possible. Hold it firmly in place until the glue begins to harden.

3 Glue a layer of moss to the hay collar so that it also extends to cover the rim of the pot.

4 Cut the rose heads from their stems and glue them on to the moss, leaving enough room for the candle. Fill the gaps with foliage. If you are using miniature roses, add them after the foliage. Half-fill the pot with moss, pressing it down well to make a base for the candle. Sprinkle the moss with rose-perfumed oil. Finally, push the candle into the terracotta pot.

HYDRANGEA CANDLE RING

· · ·

MATERIALS

· · ·

copper or steel garland ring

· · ·

hay or moss

· · ·

silver reel (rose) wire

· · ·

4 plastic candle holders

· · ·

4 candles

· · ·

glue gun and glue sticks

· · ·

scissors

· · ·

.91 wires

· · ·

dried hydrangeas

· · ·

dried Achillea filipendulina

· · ·

dried pink roses

· · ·

dried peonies

· · ·

green moss

· · ·

mossing (floral) pins'

The radiant gold of Achillea filipendulina *has a stunning impact on this display.*

Pink roses, hydrangeas, achillea and peonies make a stunning summer table decoration, and the large flowerheads will cover the garland base very quickly. Plastic candle holders are available from florists; remember never to leave burning candles unattended.

1 Cover the garland ring with hay or moss (see Techniques). Push in the candleholders at evenly spaced intervals, then add the candles to check they stand straight. Remove the candles and glue the holders to the ring. Trim and wire the hydrangeas in small bunches (see Techniques). Push the wires into the ring and glue in place, covering both the inside and outside of the ring.

2 Cut the achillea stems to about 5 cm (2 in), push them directly into the ring and glue in place.

3 Add the roses and peonies in the same way, handling them gently. Steam the roses if necessary (see Techniques).

4 Fill small gaps with green moss, attaching it with mossing (floral) pins. Glue the candles into the candleholders.

This lovely candle-lit ring of summer flowers doesn't take long to make but looks very impressive.

WOODLAND CANDLE RING

· · ·

MATERIALS

· · ·

copper or steel garland ring

· · ·

glue gun and glue sticks

· · ·

offcuts of plastic foam for dried
flowers

· · ·

4 small terracotta pots

· · ·

sphagnum moss

· · ·

silver reel (rose) wire

· · ·

.91 wires

· · ·

preserved (dried) oak leaves

· · ·

twigs

· · ·

dried eucalyptus seed heads

· · ·

dried fungi

· · ·

fir cones

· · ·

dark green moss

· · ·

mossing (floral) pins

· · ·

4 candles

*Pile the woodland materials
around the pots to create a
natural display.*

Here, a copper or steel garland ring is flattened to form the circular base for an autumnal table decoration. Preserved (dried) oak leaves are used to cover the ring then fungi, twigs, fir cones and seed heads are added on top, as on a woodland floor. Never leave the lit candles unattended.

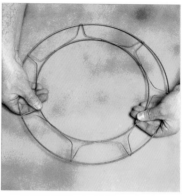

1 Push or pull the triangular wires of the ring towards each other, working all the way round, to flatten the ring.

2 Lay the ring on the clear work surface and flatten it out completely with your fingers.

3 Glue a small piece of foam under the ring. Glue a pot on top so that at least one of the wires crosses the centre of the foam, changing the angle of the wire if necessary. Space all four pots evenly around the ring.

4 Cover the ring with plenty of sphagnum moss, holding it in place with silver reel (rose) wire. The moss needs to be about 2.5 cm (1 in) thick. Pay particular attention to the base of the ring, making sure that the foam base and the area around the pots are well covered.

5 Centre-wire bunches of oak leaves, then push the wires into the moss base. They should not go through the ring but run along its length. Fill each section between the pots, using plenty of oak leaves.

6 Repeat with wired bundles of twigs, adding one bundle next to each pot. Add a second bundle of twigs to cross the first. If the wire is not long enough to hold the bundle firmly in place, use a glue gun to secure it. Add the other materials in the same way, gluing or wiring them in place to fill the spaces.

7 Fill small gaps with green moss using mossing (floral) pins. Place candles in the pots and pack them with moss.

Eucalyptus seed heads make an attractive addition to the other woodland materials.

HOP FLOWER CANDLE RING

· · ·

MATERIALS

· · ·

knife

· · ·

*10 cm (4 in) diameter plastic
foam ball*

· · ·

saucer

· · ·

*5 cm (2 in) thick beeswax
candle*

· · ·

scissors

· · ·

*dried hop bine (vine), with
about 50 hop flowers*

· · ·

6 sprigs bay leaves

*This delightful candle ring
would make an unusual
table centrepiece.*

Dried hop flowers have a delicate, translucent beauty that perfectly matches the golden honey tones of a beeswax candle. Sprigs of subtle green bay leaves, placed at regular intervals, give the design a more structured look. The fresh bay leaves will dry naturally to make a long-lasting decoration you can use again and again. Extinguish the candle before it reaches the level of the ring.

1 Cut the foam ball in half, then carefully cut a 2.5 cm (1 in) thick slice off one side.

2 Place the foam disc in a saucer. Fix the candle in the middle by gently pushing it into the centre of the foam.

3 Cut the hop flowers off the bine (vine), leaving them in their clusters where possible. Push the stalks into the foam, covering it completely.

4 Insert the sprigs of bay leaves into the foam, placing them decoratively at regular intervals around the ring.

STARFISH AND ROSE TABLE DECORATION

· · ·

9 small dried starfish

· · ·

.71 wires

· · ·

*church candle, 7.5 x 22.5 cm
(3 x 9 in)*

· · ·

*plastic foam ring for dried
flowers, 7.5 cm (3 in) diameter*

· · ·

scissors

· · ·

reindeer moss

· · ·

40 dried rose heads

*The cream roses complement
the colour of the candle and
contrast is provided by the
apricot colour and strong
geometric shape of the small
dried starfish.*

This is an alternative decoration for a large church candle using dried rose heads and starfish. The result is a table centre decoration with a seaside feel. This is a simple and quick decoration to make, but is very effective nonetheless.

1 Double leg mount all the starfish individually through one arm with .71 wires to extend their overall length. Cut the wires to approximately 2.5 cm (1 in) in length and put to one side.

2 Position the candle in the centre of the plastic foam ring. Make 2 cm (¾ in) long hairpins from cut lengths of .71 wires. Use these to pin the reindeer moss around the edge of the ring.

3 Group the wired starfish into sets of three and position each group equidistant from the others around the foam ring. Push their wires into the foam to secure.

4 Cut the stems of the dried rose heads to about 2.5 cm (1 in) and push the stems into the foam to form two continuous tightly packed rings of flowers around the candle.

POT-POURRI RING

· · ·

MATERIALS

· · ·

glue gun and glue sticks

· · ·

20 cm (8 in) diameter dried stem ring base

· · ·

115 g (4 oz) pot-pourri

· · ·

2–3 dried rosebuds

· · ·

a little dried sea lavender

· · ·

scissors

· · ·

silver reel (rose) wire

· · ·

wire-cutters or strong scissors

· · ·

.71 florist's wire

· · ·

4 cm (1½ in) wide satin ribbon

Place the ring away from strong light. If it fades and loses some of its fragrance, glue on a few more petals and sprinkle the decoration – but not the ribbon – with a few drops of pot-pourri oil, or an essential oil such as neroli.

This pretty, Victorian-style ring is very simple to make, using a glue gun to attach the scented pot-pourri to a ready-made twig base. A small posy of dried rosebuds and sea lavender, tied with ribbon, completes the effect. The long-lasting flowers make this an ideal gift; when it begins to lose its fragrance, sprinkle the ring with a few drops of pot-pourri oil, avoiding the ribbon.

1 Apply glue to the dried stem ring a little at a time. Leave to cool for a few seconds, then press some pot-pourri on to the glue.

2 Continue all around the ring until the top is completely covered inside and outside. Fill any gaps by applying more glue and pot-pourri. Save the most colourful pot-pourri petals to glue on top.

3 Make a small posy out of the dried rosebuds and sea lavender. Trim the stems short and bind with silver reel (rose) wire. Cut a florist's wire in half, then bend into a U-shape. Loop the wire over the posy stems and press into the top of the ring. Place the ribbon around the top of the ring next to the posy so that it hides the stems and binding wire. Tie in a bow and trim the ends diagonally to prevent fraying.

FLORAL CHANDELIER
· · ·

MATERIALS
· · ·

copper or steel garland ring

· · ·

glue gun and glue sticks

· · ·

offcuts of plastic foam for dried
flowers

· · ·

4 small terracotta pots

· · ·

sphagnum moss

· · ·

silver reel (rose) wire

· · ·

strong florist's wires

· · ·

dried blue and pink larkspur

· · ·

dried orange roses

· · ·

dried Achillea ptarmica

· · ·

dried peonies

· · ·

mossing (floral) pins

· · ·

dark green moss

· · ·

rope

· · ·

4 candles

*This mix of flowers will keep
its colour for a long time, but
you may need to replace the
moss after a few months.*

This unusual chandelier is designed to hang fairly low, so no flowers are added to the base. Hold it up every so often while you are making it to see how it looks from that angle. The flowers look enchanting in the candlelight; remember never to leave the chandelier unattended when lit.

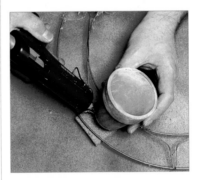

1 Flatten the garland ring by pushing or pulling the triangular wires towards each other. Glue a small piece of foam under the ring and to one of the pots, so that at least one of the wires crosses the centre of the foam; change the angle of the wire if necessary. Attach all four pots in the same way, spacing them evenly around the ring.

2 Wrap sphagnum moss around the ring, holding it in place with silver reel (rose) wire. The moss needs to be about 2.5 cm (1 in) thick. Pay particular attention to the base of the ring, making sure that the foam base and the area around the pots are covered.

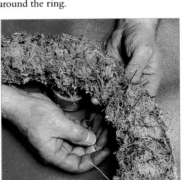

3 To create a hanging loop, push both ends of a strong wire through the ring, between two pots on the inner edge. Make sure that it crosses the ring frame under the moss. Twist the ends together and tuck into the moss. Repeat at even intervals to make four loops for hanging.

4 Centre-wire bunches of larkspur, roses and achillea. Push the wire into the moss frame. Angle the flowers so that they are pointing from the inside of the frame to the outside.

The chandelier will look dramatic when lit, and should last a fair while with such thick candles.

5 Continue to add these three materials, criss-crossing them. Place them in the same order in each quarter of the ring, to give balance to the design.

6 Cut the stems off the peonies and glue the heads in place. Using mossing (floral) pins, attach the dark green moss to the ring, filling any gaps. Attach four hanging ropes to the wire loops. Fit the candles into the pots, wedging them in place with foam and moss.

WINTER CHANDELIER

· · ·

MATERIALS

· · ·

dried oranges

· · ·

gold spray paint

· · ·

knife

· · ·

small screwdriver

· · ·

.91 wires

· · ·

glue gun and glue sticks

· · ·

moss

· · ·

starfish

· · ·

rope

· · ·

ready-made hop bine (vine) or twig garland

· · ·

green moss

· · ·

4 florist's candle holders

· · ·

4 candles

Starfish, dried oranges and moss make very unusual decorations.

This quirky chandelier consists of a moss-covered ring, from which hang gold-sprayed dried oranges decorated with gold starfish. To dry the oranges, place them on a wire rack over a stove or in an airing cupboard for several weeks until they are very hard. Remember to never leave a burning candle unattended.

1 Spray the oranges with gold paint. Cut them in half and make a hole in each half with a screwdriver. Push the two ends of a bent wire through the hole, to make a hanging loop. Turn the orange over and bend the ends of the wire up, to prevent the loop from falling out.

2 Using a glue gun, coat the inside of the orange with glue and push moss into the open space, until you have completely filled it up.

3 Take a starfish. Place glue on the moss and around the edge of the orange, where the starfish touches it. Hold in place until the glue sets. Dab a little glue on two or three more starfish and place them on the top and sides of the orange.

4 Bend the top and bottom of a long wire and hang the orange on one end. Spray it gently and carefully with gold paint, so that it provides a frosting rather than solid colour, allowing a little of the orange colour to show through.

5 Tie four lengths of rope firmly to the ring, so that the chandelier hangs horizontally. At this stage, keep the ropes fairly long so that you can adjust them afterwards.

The whole chandelier is brought together by the gold frosting on the ring and the rope.

6 Push a handful of green moss on to the ring between two of the ropes. Make a small hole in the centre of the moss with your fingers.

7 Put some glue in the hole and push a candle holder in, keeping it straight. Put a candle into the holder. Add the oranges when the chandelier is positioned.

HEARTS, STARS AND OTHER SHAPED WREATHS

• • •

*A heart-shaped wreath makes a lovely, romantic
gift for someone special, to be kept and treasured
as a long-lasting decoration. Experiment with
other unusual shapes such as stars, crescents,
triangles, diamonds and squares.*

INTRODUCTION

. . .

*Above: Scented Rosebud
Heart*

*Below: Willow and
Feather Star*

In addition to the normal circular wreaths and garlands, it is easy to make a wide variety of shapes. Hearts are extremely appealing and are really just a variation of the circular shape. Stars are made from straight twigs or stems tied together in groups of three, and this chapter also shows you how to create crescent, diamond, square, triangular, club and spade shapes.

Of all shapes, the heart must surely be the most universal. Symbolic of love and affection, a heart-shaped wreath conveys a special message to its recipient. Although the classic colour for a floral heart is red, there is no reason why hearts of all colours cannot be used. The hearts in this chapter range from ornamental cherry blossom, glossy red cranberries and sophisticated roses to dogwood twigs, dried yellow rosebuds, lavender, rosemary and golden stalks of wheat. Dried heart wreaths make excellent gifts as most are long-lasting and robust.

Star shapes make excellent wall decorations, and are an even more robust shape than hearts. A star is a good shape to choose if you have straight materials such as long twigs, which may not be pliable enough to bend into a circular ring. More supple materials can also be used, as in the willow and feather star and the eucalyptus star. For added decoration, the twigs or stalks can be bound together using twine, raffia or ribbon, depending on the effect you wish to create.

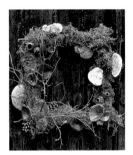

Above: Geometric Garland

Left: Woodland Heart

The crescent, diamond, square, triangular, club and spade projects in this chapter can also be achieved easily, and are interesting variations to try.

Quite apart from any other consideration, making these shapes is an excellent exercise in taping and wiring techniques. It teaches valuable lessons about the versatility of stay wires in achieving relatively complex shapes, and how the choice of material affects the form. If you want to start with something extremely simple, begin with the lavender diamond. The other shapes may take some practice to perfect, as you will encounter an increasing number of factors to take into account to achieve a successful display. It is particularly important to grade the size of materials for practical considerations such as decorating difficult corners, and to emphasize the outline of shapes.

Many of the shaped wreaths in this chapter use a single type of material in one colour, giving the wreath its own distinctive texture and reinforcing the shape of the wreath. The lavender diamond, for example, has scented blue lavender spires used directionally to emphasize its simple shape. The outline of the spade is formed from pale brown, oval poppy seed heads with distinctive star-shaped crowns and a lovely grey bloom. Bulbous, ribbed nigella seed heads in pale green and burgundy stripes define the shape of the club wreath. The scented rosebud heart shows perfectly how a simple idea – tightly packed red rosebuds – can create a very striking design.

Below: Cranberry Heart

173

UNDERWATER HEART

· · ·

For an unusual decoration, tie a raffia-covered heart to woody stems in a glass vase so that the glass magnifies the shape. Make other hearts to hang amongst the flowering branches and repeat the image. Ornamental cherries flower in the spring but you could equally well use other attractive branches such as pussy willow.

MATERIALS

· · ·

wire-cutters

· · ·

30 cm (12 in) garden wire

· · ·

raffia

· · ·

ornamental cherry blossom

· · ·

glass vase

Raffia is a natural material that is quite happy under water, and this also magnifies the heart.

1 Make a hook at each end of the wire, then link the hooks together. Make a dip in the middle of the wire for the top of the heart shape.

2 Starting at the dip and leaving a tail free for tying at the end, begin to bind the wire with raffia. Keep the raffia strips close together.

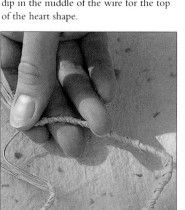

3 Take your time to bind the raffia densely all around the heart, pulling it taut as you go. Ensure that the wire is completely covered.

4 When you get back to the top, tie the ends of raffia together firmly, then make a bow. Cut the cherry blossom branches to a length suitable for the vase. Tie the branches in a bunch with raffia, then tie on the heart. Place the whole arrangement in the vase.

CRANBERRY HEART
· · ·

MATERIALS

· · ·

wire-cutters

· · ·

1 m (1 yd) garden wire

· · ·

1 large punnet cranberries

· · ·

silver reel (rose) wire

· · ·

raffia

Cranberries retain their shiny brightness for several weeks, though as the berries dry they will shrink a little.

Glossy red cranberries make a stunning decoration, bound with natural raffia. The berries are threaded like beads on to two pieces of wire, which are then placed together to create a double layer. The rich colour is ideal for a winter decoration, when the cranberries are in season.

1 Cut the garden wire in half and make a small hook at one end. Thread cranberries on to the other end. When the wire is full, make another hook and join the two together. Repeat with the other piece of wire.

2 Bend both circles into heart shapes. Put one heart shape inside the other and bind them together at top and bottom with silver reel (rose) wire.

3 Bind the hearts together all round with raffia, passing the raffia between the cranberries. Use the raffia to make a hanging loop at the top.

WOODLAND HEART

. . .

MATERIALS

. . .

secateurs (pruning shears)

. . .

pliable branches (eg buddleia)

. . .

*heavy-gauge silver reel (rose)
wire*

. . .

seagrass string

. . .

variegated trailing ivy

. . .

red berries

. . .

tree ivy

. . .

white rose

. . .

gold twine

*Red berries add a special final
touch to this simple woodland
heart wreath.*

Gently bend branches from the garden into a heart shape, then decorate it with trailing ivy and red berries for a very natural woodland effect. A small posy of ivy leaves and a single white rose is the perfect finishing touch; gild the leaves with gold spray if desired. Hang the heart on the front door to welcome guests to a winter party.

1 Cut six lengths of pliable branches about 70 cm (28 in) long. Wire three together at one end. Repeat with the other three. Cross the two bundles over at the wired end. Wire the bunches together at the cross-over point.

2 Holding the crossed, wired ends with one hand, ease the long end round and down very gently, so the branches don't snap. Repeat with the other side, to form a heart shape. Wire the bottom end of the heart.

3 Cover the wiring with seagrass string at top and bottom. Make a hanging loop at the top of the heart.

4 Twine trailing ivy around the heart shape. Add berries. Make a posy of tree ivy and a white rose, tied with gold twine. Wire the posy at the top of the heart.

SCENTED ROSEBUD HEART

· · ·

MATERIALS

· · ·

wire-cutters

· · ·

60 cm (24 in) garden wire

· · ·

*2 m (2 yd) purple ribbon,
1 cm (½ in) wide*

· · ·

glue gun and glue sticks

· · ·

25 dried rosebuds

*This heart-shaped
hanger could also be used
as a romantic gift for
Valentine's Day.*

Make this lovely little heart to hang inside a wardrobe door or as a 'token of affection'. Choose rosebuds with a strong scent or, alternatively, sprinkle a few drops of a suitable essential oil on them before you make up the heart – the oil shouldn't get on the ribbon or it may discolour.

1 Make a hook at each end of the length of garden wire. Bend it into a heart shape and join it at the bottom by linking the hooks.

2 Starting at the middle point, bind the heart with ribbon.

3 When you get back to the beginning, make a loop for hanging and secure it with a spot of glue.

4 Using a glue gun, attach the rosebuds to the heart shape.

DOGWOOD HEART

· · ·

MATERIALS

· · ·

*generous bundle of dogwood
shoots (*Cornus alba*)*

· · ·

silver reel (rose) wire

· · ·

secateurs (pruning shears)

· · ·

raffia

*Young dogwood shoots are
particularly prominent in early
spring, before the shrub
produces its foliage.*

The early spring shoots of dogwood are a lovely burgundy colour. Bend them gently into a simple heart shape, decorated with natural raffia, for a country look that would fit in well with a modern interior. Use the shoots as soon as possible after cutting while they are full of sap and still pliable.

1 Select two bundles of five large, long shoots. Very carefully, bend each bundle into a large U-shape, easing the shoots to avoid snapping them.

2 Hold the two U-shapes at right angles to each other to create a heart shape. Using silver reel (rose) wire, bind the shapes together where they cross, easing the dogwood into position.

3 Join the bottom point of the heart with wire. Once you have established the shape, you may want to re-wire all the joints to hold them firmly in place. Trim any very long ends with secateurs (pruning shears).

4 Build on the basic shape, thickening it by adding finer and shorter shoots to the top, fixing them in place with wire. These shoots will be more pliable than the original, larger ones.

5 Bind all the joints with raffia, covering the wire. Trim all the ends to neaten.

BEECH LEAF AND
DRIED ROSE HEART
. . .

MATERIALS
. . .
wire-cutters
. . .
75 cm (30 in) garden wire
. . .
florist's tape (stem-wrap tape)
. . .
silver reel (rose) wire
. . .
sprigs of preserved beech leaves
. . .
12 dried yellow rosebuds

*Green beech makes a lovely
contrast to the golden colour
of these tiny rosebuds.*

Decorate a simple wire heart shape with preserved (dried) beech leaves and dried rosebuds to make a long-lasting gift or decoration. Yellow rosebuds are used here but you could equally well use red, white or pink rosebuds.

1 Make a hook at each end of the garden wire. Bend the wire into a circle, hooking the ends together. Bind the wire circle with florist's tape (stem–wrap tape).

2 Bend the circle into a heart shape.

3 Using silver reel (rose) wire, attach the beech sprigs to the heart shape. Bend the sprigs to follow the shape as you wire them.

4 Cut 12 lengths of silver reel (rose) wire 5 cm (2 in) long and pass each one through the base of a dried rosebud. Twist the ends together.

5 Wire the yellow
rosebuds to the heart,
tucking in the ends at
the back.

*This appealing heart shape
makes a delightful gift and a
lasting decoration for anywhere
in the house.*

LAVENDER LINEN HEART
. . .

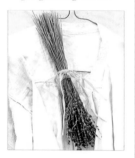

The strong scent of lavender will deter moths, as well as perfuming linen cupboards and wardrobes beautifully.

A lavender-covered wire heart is a charming "token of affection" and a welcome change to the perennially popular lavender bag. Raffia, dyed in a variety of colours, is available from a good florist's.

1 Fold the wire in half then in half again. Make a hook at one end and hook into the loop at the other end. Bend a dip in the top to form a heart shape.

2 Bind the heart with the blue-dyed raffia. Start at the bottom, working round the heart. When the heart is fully covered, tie the ends together.

3 Starting at the dip at the top, bind three stalks of lavender to the heart, with the heads pointing inwards and downwards. Continue to bind the lavender in bunches of three, working down the heart. When you reach the bottom, repeat for the other side.

4 For the bottom, make a larger bunch of lavender and glue in position with the flowerheads pointing upwards. Trim the stalks close to the heads.

FRESH ROSEMARY HEART

• • •

Long stems of rosemary make a simple decoration with a distinctive fresh scent that is very long-lasting. The fresh leaves will dry naturally if you hang the wreath away from any moisture. The scent of rosemary is very uplifting and is widely used in aromatherapy.

MATERIALS

• • •

wire-cutters

• • •

1 m (1 yd) garden wire

• • •

.71 florist's wires

• • •

12 long stems rosemary

Rosemary lasts well out of water, and can even be left to dry so that the wreath becomes an everlasting and subtly fragrant decoration.

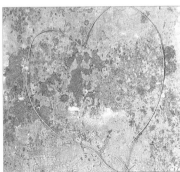

1 Make a hook at each end of the garden wire. Bend the wire into a heart shape, and join it together by hooking the ends into each other.

2 Starting at the top of the heart, wire a stem of rosemary to one side so that the leafy top points into the middle. Repeat on the other side. Wire more stems of rosemary down both sides. Add in extra stems as necessary.

HEART OF WHEAT
. . .

MATERIALS
. . .
scissors
. . .
heavy-gauge garden wire
. . .
florist's tape (stem-wrap tape)
. . .
silver reel (rose) wire
. . .
large bundle of wheat

*Fashioning simple decorations
out of wheat is a traditional
country custom, and very
satisfying to do.*

Make this endearing "token of affection" at harvest-time, perhaps for a delightful decoration to place on a kitchen wall or dresser. It is quite robust and should last for many years. You can make the base any size you wish.

1 Cut three long lengths of wire and bend them into a heart shape. Twist the ends together at the bottom.

2 Use florist's tape (stem-wrap tape) to cover the wire.

3 Using silver reel (rose) wire, bind together enough small bunches of wheat to cover the wire heart densely. Leave a short length of wire at each end.

4 Starting at the bottom, tape the first bunch of wheat stalks to the heart.

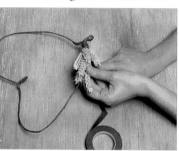

5 Tape the second bunch further up the heart shape, behind the first. Continue to tape the bunches until the whole heart is covered.

6 For the bottom, wire together about six bunches of wheat stalks, twist the wires together and wire them to the heart. Neaten with florist's tape (stem-wrap tape).

SPICY STAR WALL
DECORATION
. . .

MATERIALS
. . .
15 cinnamon sticks, 30 cm
(12 in) long
. . .
raffia
. . .
scissors
. . .
75 lavender stems
. . .
ribbon

*If a Christmas look is
required, substitute dried fruit
slices and gilded seed heads for
the lavender. Similarly, any
sturdy straight twigs can be
used instead of cinnamon.*

This star-shaped wall decoration is constructed from groups of long cinnamon sticks. It is embellished with bunches of lavender to add colour, texture, contrast and a scent which mixes with the warm, spicy smell of the cinnamon.

Its construction requires a bit of patience but is a simple matter of binding the materials together. Take care when handling the cinnamon as it can be brittle.

1 Separate the cinnamon sticks into five groups of three. Interlace the ends of two groups of sticks to form a point and secure firmly by tying them together with raffia. Trim the ends of the raffia.

2 Continue interlacing and binding together groups of cinnamon sticks to create a star-shaped framework. Also, bind together the sticks where they cross each other to make the frame rigid.

3 Separate the lavender into bunches of 15 stems each. Turn the star shape so that the binding knots are at the back and attach the bunches of lavender to the front of the frame, using raffia at the cross points of the cinnamon sticks.

4 When all the lavender bunches have been secured, make a small bow from the ribbon and tie it to the decoration at the bottom crossing point of the cinnamon sticks.

WILLOW AND FEATHER STAR

· · ·

MATERIALS

· · ·

secateurs (pruning shears)

· · ·

18 willow sticks

· · ·

scissors

· · ·

raffia

· · ·

high-tack glue

· · ·

*about 40 hen pheasant's
feathers*

*Two raffia-tied feathers add
the finishing touch to each
point of the star.*

Pliable willow sticks, or withies, make excellent wreaths and are often used in
wreath bases. Here two stick triangles are assembled into a more unusual star
shape, bound with raffia. For an enchanting effect, decorate the star with small,
delicate feathers.

1 Using secateurs (pruning shears), cut
the willow sticks down to 40 cm (16 in).
Lay three bundles of three sticks flat on a
work surface to form a triangle. Bind the
cross-over points securely with raffia.

2 Repeat to make a second triangle,
using the rest of the willow sticks. Lay
one triangle on top of the other to form a
star. Using raffia, bind the star together at
all the points where the triangles cross.

3 Trim the ends of the sticks close to the
raffia to neaten the shape.

4 Using high-tack glue, stick the
feathers to the inner hexagon of the
star, wedging them between the willow
sticks. Tie pairs of feathers in V-shapes
with raffia, and glue to the points of
the star.

EUCALYPTUS STAR

· · ·

MATERIALS

· · ·

secateurs (pruning shears)

· · ·

12 willow sticks

· · ·

silver reel (rose) wire

· · ·

small-leafed eucalyptus

Bushy blue spruce could be used to complement a frosty winter look.

The scented blue-green leaves of eucalyptus make a lovely, natural-looking star to display indoors or outdoors. The feathery eucalyptus branches are supported by a strong willow base, wired together. The leaves will dry naturally and retain their colour to make a long-lasting decoration.

1 Cut the willow sticks to about 60 cm (24 in). Place them in pairs and wire together at each end, using silver reel (rose) wire. Wire three pairs of sticks together to form a triangle. Repeat with the other three pairs.

2 Place one triangle over the other to make a star shape. Wire them together at all the points where the triangles cross.

3 Wire pieces of eucalyptus to the willow to cover the star, creating a feathery effect.

CRESCENT MOON WREATH

• • •

MATERIALS

· · ·

35 Craspedia globosa *heads*

· · ·

scissors

· · ·

.38 silver wires

· · ·

1 bunch dried linseed

· · ·

florist's tape (stem-wrap tape)

· · ·

.71 wires

This novelty decoration is designed to be hung on the wall of a nursery or child's bedroom. The golden-yellow of *Craspedia globosa* and the pale gold sheen of the linseed seed heads give the decoration a luminosity which children will love.

It is made like a garland headdress, on a stay wire but shaped to the outline of a crescent rather than a circle.

1 Cut the *Craspedia globosa* heads to a stem length of approximately 2 cm (¾ in) and double leg mount them on .38 silver wires. Split the dried linseed into very small bunches, each approximately 4 cm (1¾ in) long, and double leg mount them on .38 wires. Tape all the wired materials with the florist's tape (stem-wrap tape). Create a stay wire about 60 cm (24 in) long from the .71 wire.

2 Cover the stay wire with florist's tape (stem-wrap tape). Bend the stay wire into the outline of a crescent shape, taking care to ensure an even arc and pointed ends.

3 At one open end of the stay wire, tape on a bunch of linseed, followed by a small head of the *Craspedia globosa* slightly overlapping. Use the smaller heads of the *Craspedia globosa* at the pointed ends of the crescent and the larger heads at its centre. As you get towards the centre of the crescent, increase the width of the line of materials by adding material to the sides of the wire. Decrease the width again as you work towards the far point.

4 When the outside edge of the crescent outline has been completed, repeat the process on the inner edge but this time working from the bent point of the crescent down towards the open end of the stay wire. When the inner wire has been decorated, join the two open ends of the stay wire by taping them together, then cut off any excess wires and tape over their ends. This joint will be hidden by the dried materials.

To make the crescent shape accurately – narrower at its points – requires a degree of skill and like all wired decorations, time and patience.

POPPY SPADE WREATH

· · ·

MATERIALS

· · ·

.71 wires

· · ·

florist's tape (stem-wrap tape)

· · ·

scissors

· · ·

*50 stems dried poppy seed
heads*

· · ·

.38 silver wires

*It is important to tape the
poppy seed heads closely
together so that they can rest
against each other and not
"flop" down.*

1 Make a stay wire from .71 wire on
which the decoration can be built.
Cover with florist's tape (stem-wrap tape).
Form the stay wire into a spade shape
about 22 cm (8¾ in) high with the two
ends of the wire meeting in a line at the
bottom of the shape.

2 Cut the stems of the poppy seed heads
to a length of approximately 2.5 cm
(1 in) and double leg mount the
individual poppy seed heads on .38 silver
wires, then tape the wired stems with
florist's tape (stem–wrap tape) to hide
the wire.

3 Starting at the pointed
top of the shape, tape
the poppy seed heads to
the stay wire starting with
the smallest. Slightly
overlap the seed heads to
achieve a continuous line.
The size of the heads
should be increased as you
work towards the bulbous
part of the shape, after
which the heads should be
decreased. When you have
completed one side, repeat
the whole process on the
opposite side, again
starting from the point at
the top. Tape the two ends
of the stay wire together
with tape.

LAVENDER DIAMOND WREATH

. . .

MATERIALS
. . .
.71 wires
. . .
florist's tape (stem-wrap tape)
. . .
scissors
. . .
105 stems dried lavender
. . .
.38 silver wires

Ensure that all the lavender spires point in the same direction to give this simple wreath maximum impact.

1 Make a stay wire from .71 wire on which the decoration can be built. Cover with florist's tape (stem-wrap tape). Form the stay wire into a diamond shape about 22 cm (8¾ in) high with the two ends meeting at the bottom point.

2 Cut the lavender to an overall length of approximately 5 cm (2 in) and group it in threes. Double leg mount these groups with .38 wires, then tape the 35 wired groups with florist's tape (stem-wrap tape).

3 Start at the top point of the diamond shape and attach the groups of lavender by taping around their wired stems and the stay wire. Slightly overlap one group with the next to achieve a continuous line around one half of the shape, finishing at the bottom open end of the stay wire. Start covering the second half of the diamond shape from the bottom open end of the stay wire. When covered, tape the two open ends together.

NIGELLA CLUB WREATH

· · ·

MATERIALS

· · ·

.71 wires

· · ·

florist's tape (stem-wrap tape)

· · ·

scissors

· · ·

*57 stems dried nigella seed
heads of similar size*

· · ·

.38 silver wires

*This wreath makes an eye-
catching and fun decoration.*

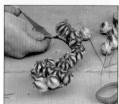

1 Make a stay wire from
.71 wire on which the
decoration can be built.
Cover with florist's tape
(stem-wrap tape). Form
the stay wire into a club
shape about 22 cm (8¾ in)
high with the two ends of
the wire meeting in a line
at the centre at the bottom
of the shape.

2 Cut the stems of the
nigella to a length of
approximately 2.5 cm
(1 in) and double leg
mount the individual
nigella seedheads on .38
silver wires. Tape the
wired stems with florist's
tape (stem-wrap tape).

3 Starting at the
beginning of the stay
wire, tape the wired heads
of nigella to the stay wire.
Slightly overlap the nigella
heads to achieve a
continuous line. Continue
until the stay wire is
covered and then join the
two ends of the wire
together by taping.

GEOMETRIC GARLAND
· · ·

Most garlands are round, but they can also be square or triangular. Experiment with different shapes created with canes or sticks – they do not have to be completely straight to create an interesting variation.

MATERIALS
· · ·
strong canes or sticks
· · ·
strong florist's wires
· · ·
pliers
· · ·
glue gun and glue sticks
· · ·
moss
· · ·
silver reel (rose) wire
· · ·
twigs
· · ·
.91 wires
· · ·
dried fungi
· · ·
fir cones

If you make a triangular frame, the resulting garland is even more unusual.

1 If the canes or sticks are thin, wire 5–8 together to make one stronger length for each side of the frame. Use pliers to twist the wire around the ends. Make a square frame, tying the canes or sticks in each corner with a wire. Add a dab of glue to the wires to fix them firmly.

2 Cover the frame with moss, holding it in place with silver reel (rose) wire. Try to keep an even amount of moss on all sides and avoid leaving any gaps. Make the base secure, as this is what the remaining material will be attached to.

3 When the frame is completely covered with moss, tie the twigs on to it with wire. Add as many as you think look good, remembering what materials you have to come. Then glue the fungi and fir cones in position, placing them in small groups. Hide any wires that show with extra moss.

SPECIAL
OCCASIONS

• • •

Celebrate special occasions with glorious garlands, circles, wreaths and swags. From Valentine's Day through to Thanksgiving and Christmas, this chapter contains festive inspirations for the whole year, as well as stunning ideas for wedding receptions and summer garden parties.

INTRODUCTION
· · ·

Above: Mother's Day Wreath

Below: Advent Candle Ring

Traditionally flowers go hand in hand with special occasions – what would Mother's Day or a wedding be without celebratory flowers? Throughout the calendar year, from Valentine's Day to Christmas, the flower arranger has opportunity after opportunity to express his or her creativity.

Heart-shaped wreaths are perfect for Valentine's Day, and the hearts in this chapter are especially romantic, being made from roses. Mother's Day and Easter are associated with fresh springtime flowers, so celebrate these seasonal occasions with pear blossom, pussy willow and daffodil wreaths. Harvest Festival and Thanksgiving conjure up images of the bounty of nature – fruit, vegetables and ears of corn – and there are some beautiful dried wreaths in this chapter as a reminder of summer days gone by.

For big events like weddings, the flower arranger is presented with a real challenge. Not only do you need the necessary skills to design, arrange and wire the materials, you also need the skills to organize the project properly by making

Above: Bridesmaid's Circlet

Left: Table Swag

a series of important decisions correctly. You need to decide exactly what you are going to make, and calculate the quantities of flowers and foliage necessary in order to avoid buying too much or, worse, buying too little. A carefully considered timetable should be prepared for the event.

If you opt to use fresh flowers, you must decide when to order the flowers and how long the different varieties will remain in good condition. Remember, too, that some flowers may require a few days before the event to open fully. Estimate how long it will take to make each headdress, garland, swag and table decoration. Consider the time-scale available to you for working with the flowers and, to avoid all-night labouring, how many helpers you will need. Can the large arrangements be made *in situ*, or will they need to be made somewhere else and transported and, if so, how? You must also decide what other materials you will need, such as ribbon or pins.

Choosing dried flowers for wedding headdresses and garlands gives you an important time advantage because you can work at your own pace well before the event. Even so, you will need a very long, comprehensive check-list.

At Christmas, a colourful, welcoming garland on your front door sets the scene and provides the perfect festive welcome for your guests. If you're feeling nostalgic for a traditional country Christmas, try making a blue pine (spruce) garland or swag, adorned with fir cones and ribbons. More unusual garlands featured in this chapter include a luxurious circle of pomegranates, artichokes and chillies, and a wreath of tightly grouped orange clementines, berries and leaves. For an extra-festive feel to your wreaths and mantelpiece decorations, spray some of the fir cones and leaves with gold paint.

Below: Aromatic Christmas Wreath

VALENTINE'S GARLAND
· · ·

MATERIALS
· · ·
garden wire
· · ·
silver reel (rose) wire
· · ·
moss
· · ·
scissors
· · ·
small dried flowers, e.g. roses, rosebuds, lavender, bupleurum
· · ·
glue gun and glue sticks

Roses are particularly suited to this heart-shaped garland because they conjure up images of romance and fond memories.

Give this lovely miniature garland as a very special memento, which can be hung on a dresser or bedroom wardrobe. Decorate it either with roses and bupleurum or with lavender and roses. The garland is constructed on a simple wire base; you can buy these ready-made, but it is very easy to make your own.

1 Fold the garden wire in half then in half again. Bend a hook in the wire at one end and hook it into the loop in the folded wire at the other end, to make a circle. Make a dip in the top of the circle to create a heart shape.

2 Using silver reel (rose) wire, bind the wire heart with a thin layer of moss. Trim the moss to neaten the shape.

3 Trim the stems off all the flowers. Glue the flowerheads to the moss heart, working on each side in turn to keep a balance. Add the largest roses last at the top of the heart shape. Glue extra moss to fill any small gaps.

SMALL FRESH ROSE
VALENTINE'S RING
• • •

While this delightful floral circlet could be used at any time of the year, the impact created by the massed red roses makes it particularly appropriate to Valentine's Day. It can be hung on a wall or, with a candle at its centre, used as a table decoration for a romantic dinner for two.

MATERIALS
• • •

plastic foam ring,
15 cm (6 in) diameter
• • •
dark green ivy leaves
• • •
.71 wires
• • •
bun moss
• • •
20 dark red roses
• • •
scissors

If you receive a Valentine's Day bouquet of red roses, why not recycle them? After the rose blooms have fully blown open, cut down their stems for use in this circlet to extent their lives. Finally dehydrate the circlet and continue to use it as a dried flower display.

1 Soak the plastic foam ring in water. Push individual, medium-sized ivy leaves into the foam to create an even foliage outline all around the ring.

2 Make hairpin shapes out of the .71 wires and pin small pieces of bun moss on to the foam ring between the ivy leaves. Do this throughout the foliage but to a thinner density than the ivy.

3 Cut the rose stems to approximately 3.5 cm (1½ in) long and push them into the foam until the ring is evenly covered. The ivy leaves should still be visible in between the rose heads.

MOTHER'S DAY WREATH
. . .

MATERIALS
. . .

20 cm (8 in) diameter plastic foam ring

. . .

secateurs (pruning shears)

. . .

young rosemary shoots

. . .

pussy willow (Salix caprea)

. . .

pear blossom

The fragrance of rosemary awakens the senses, adding charm to this special wreath.

This special day comes at a lovely time of year when plants are making fresh new growth and there is plenty of blossom. The main ingredient of the wreath is rosemary, arranged at an angle so that it appears to flow around the ring. Add some soft grey pussy willow and delicate pear (or apple) blossom to decorate the green herb base. The scent of the rosemary makes your gift even more attractive.

1 Immerse the foam ring in water until it is completely soaked through. Cut the stems of rosemary to 15 cm (6 in).

2 Push the rosemary stems into the foam ring, placing them at an angle so that they flow around the circle in one direction. Add the pussy willow, placing most of it at the top of the inside edge for impact.

3 Insert most of the pear blossom to cover the inside edge of the ring. Add a few blossoms on the outside. Fill any gaps with spare rosemary.

EASTER WREATH

· · ·

*Whether in the church or
home, this delightful Easter
decoration will bring pleasure
to all who view it.*

Easter is a time of hope and regeneration and this bright Easter wreath visually captures these feelings. It overflows with the floral symbols of spring with daffodils and polyanthus, and contains eggs, a symbol of birth.

The vibrant colours and the flowers, arranged to look as though they are still growing, give the wreath a fresh, natural glow. There is also a touch of humour in the crossed enamel spoons.

1 Soak the foam ring in water and arrange an even covering of elaeagnus stems, approximately 7.5 cm (3 in) long, in the foam. At five equidistant positions, add groups of three polyanthus leaves.

3 Arrange the polyanthus flowers in single-coloured groups as though they are growing by pushing their stems into the plastic foam. Be sure to leave a section of the ring clear for the eggs and spoons. Cut the daffodils to a stem length of approximately 7.5 cm (3 in) and between four groups of polyanthus arrange groups of 15 daffodils, pushing their stems into the plastic foam.

2 Wire the eight pieces of bark by bending a .71 wire around the middle and twisting to achieve a tight grip. Position the pieces of bark equidistant around the ring by pushing the protruding wires into the plastic foam.

4 Bend .71 wires around the spoons and twist. In the gap left on the ring position one of the spoons, wrapping the wire ends around to the back of the ring. Twist the wires together tightly so that the spoon is embedded in the foam. Do this with both spoons, arranged so that they cross. Wrap raffia around the eggs, crossing it over underneath and tying it on the side. Bend .71 wires around the eggs, twisting the ends together gently. Arrange the remaining daffodils and polyanthus flowers around the eggs and spoons.

BRIDESMAID'S CIRCLET

. . .

MATERIALS

. . .

two .91 florist's wires

. . .

white gutta percha tape (floral tape)

. . .

scissors

. . .

spray chrysanthemums

. . .

larkspur

. . .

delphinium florets

. . .

silver reel (rose) wire

. . .

small roses

. . .

2.5 cm (1 in) wide ribbon

. . .

plant spray

A corsage, to be worn by a principal wedding guest, may be composed of similar flowers.

This pretty circlet of fresh flowers is perfect for a summer wedding in a country church. Choose the colours of the flowers and ribbon to complement the bridesmaid's dresses, adding a few darker tones, such as the deep blue larkspur shown here, to the paler colours. If you are travelling to the church, wrap the circlet lightly in tissue paper and keep it out of the sun.

1 To give the headdress more variety of colour, slender stems of dark blue larkspur and delphinium are blended with large florets, in a paler tint, cut from long spires of a similar plant. This also has the advantage of including favourite flowers from the garden without visibly denuding it.

2 To make the base of the headdress, twist two florist's wires together to form a circle. Bind the wire with gutta percha tape (floral tape), which is self-adhesive, taking it around the wire so that each strip of tape overlaps the previous one.

3 Cut the flower stems to a length of about 4 cm (1½ in). Gather them into clusters of one or two spray chrysanthemums, a short spray of larkspur and a delphinium floret. Bind the stems with a few twists of silver reel (rose) wire, then bind the cluster to the circle with the wire. Wire on a rose, more flower clusters, another rose and so on, until the circlet is complete. Tie the ribbon in a bow with long, trailing ends. Neaten the ends by cutting them at an angle. Thread silver reel (rose) wire through the back of the ribbon loop and bind the bow to the headdress. Spray the flowers with a fine mist of cool water, and keep the decoration in a cool place (such as the fridge) until the last minute.

DRIED FLOWER GARLAND HEADDRESS

• • •

MATERIALS

• • •

scissors

• • •

9 dried peonies with leaves

• • •

27 dried red roses

• • •

.71 wires

• • •

.38 silver wires

• • •

.32 silver reel (rose) wire

• • •

27 slices preserved (dried) apple

• • •

18 short sprigs dried ti tree

• • •

9 small clusters hydrangea

• • •

florist's tape (stem-wrap tape)

An advantage of using dried materials is that they can be made well in advance, which means less to worry about on the big day. There is plenty of wiring involved, but otherwise the construction is relatively straightforward.

This wedding headdress is made from dried materials in beautiful soft pale pinks, greens and lilacs with the interesting addition of apple slices. Apart from being very pretty, it will not wilt during the wedding and can, of course, be kept after the event.

1 Cut the peonies and the roses to a stem length of 2.5 cm (1 in). Double leg mount the peonies with .71 wires and the roses with .38 silver wires. Group the roses into threes and bind together using the .32 silver reel (rose) wire. Group the apple slices into threes and double leg mount them together with .71 wire. Cut the sprigs of ti tree, hydrangea clusters and eucalyptus to lengths of 5 cm (2 in) and double leg mount with .38 silver wires, grouping the ti tree and eucalyptus in twos. Cover all the wired stems with tape.

2 Have to hand the bride's head measurements. Make the stay wire on which the headdress will be built with .71 wires, ensuring its final length is approximately 4 cm (1½ in) longer than the circumference of the head.

3 Position a piece of wired eucalyptus on one end of the stay wire and wrap florist's tape (stem-wrap tape) over its stem and the stay wire, to secure them together. Then, in the same way, add in turn a hydrangea cluster, a group of roses, a peony and a group of ti tree, repeating the sequence until the stay wire is covered. Remember to leave the last 4 cm (1½ in) of the stay wire uncovered.

4 To complete the headdress, overlap the uncovered end of the stay wire with the decorated start and tape together with florist's tape (stem-wrap tape), ensuring the tape goes under the flowers so that it is not visible.

The bold nature of this headdress makes it particularly suitable for a bride.

WEDDING SWAG
• • •

Lavender combines so well with many other flowers, and is combined here with criss-crossing bunches of roses.

This pretty, soft combination is ideal for a summer wedding and can be made any length to fit the particular location. It would look very welcoming placed either side of the church door, or fixed in an arch above it; inside the church, it could be wrapped around a stone pillar. Making a loop at each end of the rope ensures that there is a fixing in the right place.

1 Cut the rope to the required length, with a little extra at each end for the hanging loops. Trim the nigella, oregano and larkspur stems to 15 cm (6 in) in length and make separate piles of each. Start at one end of the rope, tying on a small bunch of nigella with silver reel (rose) wire, to cover the hanging loop.

2 Move along the rope, covering the stems of the nigella with a small bunch of oregano, again tying it in place with wire. Repeat with the larkspur, tying the bunches on to the rope.

3 Continue to alternate these three materials. Check that when the swag is lying on a flat surface, there are no gaps along the side and try to keep the swag to an even thickness along the rope.

4 Bunch and centre-wire the lavender and roses. Add these almost at right angles to the other materials. Push the wires through the centre of the swag and twist the ends together then push the sharp ends back into the swag. Tie a bow in the ribbon and glue it to one end of the swag.

TABLE SWAG
· · ·

MATERIALS
· · ·
scissors
· · ·
gypsophila
· · ·
mimosa
· · ·
spray chrysanthemums
· · ·
silver reel (rose) wire
· · ·
*smilax (*Asparagus
asparagoides)
· · ·
dressmaker's pins
· · ·
*2.5 cm (1 in) wide satin
ribbon*

*A swag is a lovely way to
decorate a wedding or
christening reception.*

This beautiful table decoration is very impressive for a formal garden party or summer wedding, looped across the front of a long buffet table or around all four sides of a smaller table. Smilax can be ordered from florists and is very pliable to work with. To save time, make the colourful posies of flowers in advance and keep them fresh in a bowl of water until you are ready to assemble the swag.

1 Smilax, with its pliable stem and mass of bright green leaves, forms a natural garland, and makes an attractive instant decoration, even without the addition of flowers. It is usually sold to order in bundles of five stems. Keep the stem ends in water until just before you assemble the garland, and the foliage should stay fresh for several days.

2 Cut the flower stems short. Compose each posy using five or six pieces of gypsophila, two small snippings of mimosa and one or two spray chrysanthemums, according to size. Gather the stems together and bind them with silver reel (rose) wire.

3 Check the number of posies needed. As a general rule, the smaller the table the smaller the gap between the flowers. Once the posies are assembled place them in a shallow bowl of water.

4 Measure the length needed for the side drapes and mark the centre. With the stems of the first posy towards the end of one of the lengths of foliage, bind the posy to the main stem with silver reel wire. Bind on more posies in the same way, reversing the direction of the stems when you reach the centre. Repeat for the remaining lengths, but without reversing direction on the corner pieces. Pin the garland to the tablecloth, adjusting the swag so that it is equal on all sides. Pin on the corner pieces. Check that the swag hangs well. Sometimes the weight of the posies will cause it to twist, with the flowers facing inwards. If this happens, pin the swag to the tablecloth at intervals. Pin ribbon or ribbon bows to the corners and the centre of each drape.

CELEBRATION TABLE DECORATION

· · ·

A table for any celebratory lunch will not usually have much room to spare on it. In this instance there is no room for the wine cooler, and the answer is to incorporate this large but necessary piece of catering equipment within the flower arrangement.

The floral decoration is a sumptuous, textural display of gold, yellow and white flowers with green and grey foliage. The spiky surfaces of the chestnuts add a wonderful variation in texture.

MATERIALS

· · ·

plastic foam ring,
40.7 cm (16 in) diameter

· · ·

scissors

· · ·

12 stems Senecio laxifolius

· · ·

15 stems elaeagnus

· · ·

3 groups 2 chestnuts

· · ·

.71 wires

· · ·

thick gloves

· · ·

18 stems yellow roses

· · ·

10 stems cream-coloured
Eustoma grandiflorum

· · ·

10 stems solidago

· · ·

10 stems dill

The arrangement is based on a circular, plastic foam ring with the centre left open to accommodate the wine cooler. The splendid silver wine cooler is enhanced by the beauty of the flowers, and in turn its highly polished surface reflects the flowers to increase their visual impact.

1 Soak the plastic foam ring in water. Cut the senecio to a stem length of around 14 cm (5½ in) and distribute evenly around the ring, pushing the stems into the plastic foam, to create an even foliage outline. Leave the centre of the ring clear.

2 Cut the elaeagnus to a length of about 14 cm (5½ in) and distribute evenly throughout the senecio to reinforce the foliage outline, still leaving the centre of the plastic foam ring clear to eventually accommodate the wine cooler.

3 Double leg mount three groups of two chestnuts on .71 wire and cut the wire legs to about 6 cm (2¼ in). Take care, as the chestnuts are extremely prickly and it is advisable to wear heavy duty gardening gloves when handling them.

4 Still wearing your gloves, position the groups of chestnuts at three equidistant points around the circumference of the plastic foam ring, and secure by pushing the wires into the plastic foam.

5 Cut the rose stems to approximately 14 cm (5½ in) in length and arrange in staggered groups of three roses at six points around the ring, equal distances apart, pushing the stems firmly into the plastic foam.

6 Cut stems of eustoma flowerheads 12 cm (4¾ in) long from the main stem. Arrange the stems evenly in the foam. Cut the stems of solidago to a length of about 14 cm (5½ in) and distribute throughout. Finally cut the stems of fennel to about 12 cm (4¾ in) long and add evenly through the display, pushing the stems into the plastic foam.

This magnificent arrangement would make a stunning centrepiece for a wedding table.

DRIED FLOWER HORSESHOE
BABY GIFT
• • •

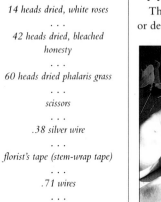

What could be nicer for new parents than to receive a floral symbol of good luck on the birth of their baby?

The whites and pale green of this dried flower horseshoe make it a perfect gift or decoration for the nursery.

1 Cut the rose stems, honesty stems and phalaris grass to approximately 2.5 cm (1 in) long. Double leg mount the roses individually on .38 silver wire, then tape. Double leg mount the phalaris heads in groups of five on .38 silver wire, and the honesty in clusters of three on .38 silver wire. Tape each group.

2 Make a stay wire approximately 30 cm (12 in) long from .71 wire on which the horseshoe will be built.

3 Form three small bows approximately 4 cm (1½ in) wide from the ribbon and bind them at their centres with .38 silver wire. Cut a 30 cm (12 in) length of ribbon and double leg mount both ends separately with .38 silver wire. This will form the handle for the horseshoe.

4 Form the stay wire into a horseshoe shape. Tape one wired end of the ribbon to one end of the stay wire. Tape one of the bows over the junction of the ribbon and stay wire, making sure it is securely in place.

5 Starting at the bow, tape the flowers and foliage to the stay wire, to its mid point, in the following repeating sequence: phalaris, rose, honesty. Tape a bow at the centre and tape the last bow and the remaining ribbon end to the other end of the stay wire. Work the flowers in the same sequence back to the centre point.

While making the horseshoe is relatively time-consuming, the effort will no doubt have created something of such sentimental value that it will be kept forever.

THANKSGIVING WREATH
. . .

MATERIALS
. . .
27 dried sunflower heads
. . .
.71 wires
. . .
*florist's tape
(stem-wrap tape)*
. . .
scissors
. . .
*30 pieces dried fungus
(various sizes)*
. . .
3 dried corn cobs
. . .
large vine circlet
. . .
raffia

Thanksgiving time conjures up images of fruit, vegetables and ears of corn. This wreath of dried flowers has corn cobs as its harvest time reference point, visually reinforced with fungus, a less obvious autumn crop, and sunflowers, which in this form serve as a reminder of summer days gone by.

1 Single leg mount individual sunflower heads on .71 wires. Tape the stems, then group in threes. Double leg mount these groups with .71 wire and tape the stems. Double leg mount the pieces of fungus with .71 wire. You may need to cut the wire so that it has a sharp end to push through the fungus and twist into a double leg mount. Do not tape these wires.

2 Group the corn cobs at the bottom of the vine circlet and push their stems between the twisted vines, crossing them over each other to form a fan shape. Secure the corn cobs to each other and to the circlet with .71 wire.

3 Attach the groups of sunflowers, evenly spaced, all around the circumference of the circlet by pushing their wires through and wrapping tightly around the vines. These sunflower groups should alternate between the outside and inside edges of the vines.

4 Attach the fungus in groups of twos and threes around the circlet, between the sunflowers and around the corn cobs. The fungus groups should have the largest piece at the bottom with progressively smaller pieces above. Secure the fungus by straddling the vine with the legs of wire and twisting them together at the back.

5 Finally form a large bow from the raffia and tie it to the wreath over the stems of the corn cobs to conceal any remaining visible wires.

The large scale of this simple but unusual combination of materials gives the wreath great visual impact.

CORN-ON-THE-COB GARLAND

. . .

MATERIALS

. . .

medium-gauge garden wire

. . .

scissors or secateurs

. . .

old wooden sieve

. . .

*dried hop stems with leaves
and flowers*

. . .

*small dried corn-on-the-cob,
with leaves*

*The spiky, textured
appearance of the corn-on-the
cob leaves helps to give this
display its rustic charm.*

Dried corn-on-the cob comes in attractive shades ranging from pale yellow to rich orange, which make a lovely Thanksgiving display. Here the base of the garland is an old wooden sieve, and dried hops add to the charming rustic effect.

1 Thread a length of wire through a hole in the sieve frame and around the wire mesh. Repeat on all four sections of the sieve where there is an existing hole.

2 Cut four short lengths of hop stems and attach the ends to the wires. Twist the wire ends together to secure. Repeat to cover the whole sieve edge.

3 Choose three corn heads of similar length and tie them together with a length of wire. Holding the cluster of corn tightly together with one hand, fold the wire over the leaves of all three cobs.

4 Twist the wire ends together. To conceal the wire, fold down a few of the corn leaves and wrap them neatly around the wire.

5 Tie the ends of the leaves with another length of wire to form a tuft. Trim excess wires and leaves.

6 Attach the groups of corn around the sieve by threading the wire through the mesh and on to the hop garland. Twist the wire ends together. Stagger the corn at regular intervals around the sieve.

7 Trim excess wires and corn leaves, but don't over-trim as this will detract from the charm of the arrangement.

The wire mesh and wooden frame of an old sieve blend perfectly with the colours and textures of the natural dried materials.

ADVENT CANDLE RING

· · ·

MATERIALS

· · ·

1 block plastic foam

· · ·

knife

· · ·

ring basket

· · ·

4 church candles

· · ·

moss

· · ·

.71 florist's wires

· · ·

dried orange slices

· · ·

secateurs (pruning shears)

· · ·

cinnamon sticks

· · ·

gold twine

· · ·

tree ivy

· · ·

Cape gooseberries

The fruits and bundles of cinnamon sticks are a delight to the eye, while giving off a rich seasonal aroma.

This is a lovely traditional way to celebrate the month before Christmas. On the first Sunday of Advent one of the candles is lit, on the second Sunday two are lit and so on until on the last Sunday all four candles are ceremoniously lit together. The creamy church candles are presented in a ring basket lined with small bundles of ivy and decorated with seasonal fruits and spices.

1 Soak the plastic foam and cut it into pieces to fit the ring basket.

2 Push the candles into the foam, spacing them equally around the ring.

3 Cover the foam with moss, pushing it well down at the sides of the basket.

4 To wire the orange slices, pass a wire through the centre, then twist the wire ends together at the outside edge. Wire the cinnamon sticks into bundles, then tie them with gold twine and pass a wire through the twine.

5 Wire the tree-ivy leaves together into small bundles.

6 Place the ivy leaves in the ring. Decorate with the orange slices and cinnamon sticks. Place Cape gooseberries on top at intervals.

An Advent candle ring makes a beautiful Christmas centrepiece.

229

PINE CHRISTMAS GARLAND
• • •

MATERIALS
• • •
copper or steel ring
• • •
moss
• • •
silver reel (rose) wire
• • •
secateurs (pruning shears)
• • •
blue pine (spruce)
• • •
dried amaranthus, dyed red
• • •
.91 wires
• • •
dried red roses
• • •
dried lavender
• • •
raffia
• • •
twigs
• • •
sweet chestnuts
• • •
fir cones
• • •
dried fungi
• • •
strong florist's wire

Blue pine (spruce) instantly evokes Christmas spirit.

In this garland, blue pine (spruce) is used fresh and left to dry out later. It releases a glorious fresh scent as you work with it and makes a magnificent Christmas decoration. Here it is used with red roses and amaranthus for a traditional look. You could also add fresh apples or tangerines for a lively, if less long-lasting, arrangement – pierce each fruit with a wire to fix it in place.

1 Cover the ring very roughly on both sides with moss – this need not be thick but should be fairly even. Secure in place by winding with silver reel (rose) wire, leaving a space of about 5 cm (2 in) between each loop.

2 Trim the blue pine (spruce) to lengths of about 15–20 cm (6–8 in). Divide into four piles and begin to tie each stem to the ring with wire, using one pile for each quarter of the ring. Work outward from the inner edge in a zigzag fashion.

3 Trim the amaranthus stems to 20 cm (8 in) and wire into four small bunches (see Techniques), leaving the wires untrimmed. Treat the roses in the same way, but cut the stems to 10 cm (4 in). In each quarter of the ring, push a bunch of roses and a bunch of amaranthus, tying the wires into the back of the ring.

4 Trim the lavender to 20 cm (8 in) and wire into four bunches. Keep a long length of wire hanging from each bunch and wind a bow of raffia around the stems. Push each wire through the blue pine (spruce) and tie to the back of the ring.

5 Wire bunches of twigs, chestnuts, fir cones and fungi. Tie bows of raffia around the bunches of twigs. Add these materials in small mixed groups, linking each group around the ring. Add a loop of strong wire to the back of the garland for hanging and tie a raffia bow at the top.

Hung outside the front door, a Christmas garland provides a festive welcome for visitors.

SPRUCE AND CONE WREATH

· · ·

MATERIALS

· · ·

.91 florist's wires

· · ·

30 cm (12 in) diameter straw wreath base

· · ·

carpet moss

· · ·

mossing (floral) pins

· · ·

secateurs (pruning shears)

· · ·

blue pine (spruce)

· · ·

12 cinnamon sticks

· · ·

6 large fir cones

· · ·

3 m (3 yd) satin ribbon, 7.5 cm (3 in) wide

· · ·

9 poppy seed heads

· · ·

sisal string

Soft blues and greens give this Christmas wreath a Scandinavian look.

The soft colour of blue pine (spruce) makes a beautiful Christmas wreath to hang on the front door. It is handsomely decorated with fir cones and cinnamon sticks, creating a rich mixture of spicy seasonal scents. Luxurious ribbon bows and frayed bows of rough sisal string give an interesting textural contrast. The wired ribbon will stand up well outdoors even in bad weather.

1 Use a length of wire to attach a small loop to the straw ring to allow you to hang the wreath. Cover the ring with carpet moss, pinning it in place with the mossing (floral) pins.

2 Cut the blue pine (spruce) into short lengths and pin them on the moss.

3 Wire the cinnamon sticks into three bundles and attach them to the garland with mossing pins. Attach wires to the base of the fir cones by twisting them around the scales. Pin them close to the cinnamon sticks. Cut the ribbon into three pieces and fold each into a double bow, using wire to secure the bows. Pin the bows over the cinnamon sticks and fir cones. Tuck the poppy seed heads into the folds of the bows and pin in place. Tie three bows with sisal string, fray the ends and pin them on to the wreath.

CHRISTMAS WREATH
WITH ARTICHOKES
· · ·

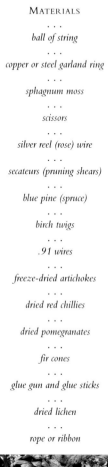

The artichokes provide dramatic shapes and texture, but you can use another dried material if they are not readily available.

This luxurious Christmas wreath combines the rich colours and textures of pomegranates, artichokes and chillies with traditional evergreen foliage and fir cones. It can be hung on a door or placed in the centre of the dining table.

1 Attach the end of the string to the larger of the two rings. Attach the moss to both sides evenly, winding the string tightly around the ring. Continue until the whole ring is covered, then tie the string firmly and trim the ends.

2 Tie the end of the silver reel (rose) wire to the ring. Snip off several sprigs of blue pine (spruce) and build up a thick garland by staggering them evenly around the ring. Secure each sprig in place by winding the wire tightly around the stem.

3 Continue to build up the blue pine (spruce) base until the whole ring is covered. Cut off the wire and twist it around itself several times on the underside of the wreath.

4 Make large loops out of birch twigs and place diagonally at intervals around the wreath. Secure with lengths of wire bent into U-shaped pins pushed firmly through the middle of the wreath.

5 Wire the larger dried materials individually (see Techniques). Begin with a group of artichokes. Push the wired stems firmly through the body of the wreath.

6 Wire the chillies in threes (see Techniques). Group them together between the artichokes in large clusters.

This full-bodied wreath makes a perfect decoration for the festive season.

7 Insert the pomegranates in clusters of at least five to balance the artichoke and chilli groups. Fill in the gaps with smaller clusters of fir cones.

8 Glue the lichen to the wreath. It is very delicate and cannot be wired. Intertwine rope or ribbon between the dried materials. Anchor it with wires folded in half to form U-shaped pins.

CLEMENTINE WREATH

· · ·

MATERIALS

· · ·

.71 wires

· · ·

27 clementines

· · ·

*plastic foam ring, approximately
30 cm (12 in) diameter*

· · ·

pyracantha berries and foliage

· · ·

ivy leaves

*The wreath will look
spectacular hung on a door or
wall, and can also be used as a
table decoration with a large
candle at its centre, or perhaps
a cluster of smaller candles of
staggered heights. The wreath
is very easy to make, but it is
heavy and if it is to be hung
on a wall or door, be sure to fix
it securely.*

This festive Christmas wreath is contemporary in its regular geometry and its bold use of materials and colours. Tightly-grouped seasonal clementines, berries and leaves are substituted for the traditional holly, mistletoe and pine. The wreath has a citrus smell, but can be made more aromatic by using bay leaves and other herbs instead of ivy.

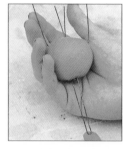

1 Push a .71 wire across and through the base of the clementine from one side to the other, and bend the two projected ends down. Bend another .71 wire to form a hairpin shape and push the ends right through the middle of the clementine so that the bend in the wire is sitting flush with the top of the fruit. Do the same to all the clementines. Cut all the projecting wires to a length of approximately 4 cm (1½ in).

2 Soak the plastic foam ring in water. Arrange the wired clementines in a tight circle on the top of the plastic ring by pushing their four projecting wire legs into the foam. Form a second ring of clementines within the first ring.

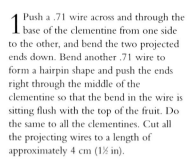

3 Cut the pyracantha into small stems of berry clusters and foliage approximately 6 cm (2¼ in) long. Push the stems into the outer side of the plastic ring and between the two rings of clementines, making sure they are evenly distributed.

4 Cut the ivy leaves into individual stems measuring approximately 7 cm (2¾ in) in length. Push the stems of the individual leaves into the plastic ring, positioning a leaf between each clementine.

YULETIDE KISSING WREATH

· · ·

MATERIALS

· · ·

newspaper

· · ·

wheat seed heads

· · ·

linseed (flax) seed heads

· · ·

artificial roses, with wire stems

· · ·

delicate evergreens (eg cypress, ivy, mistletoe, eucalyptus)

· · ·

gold spray paint

· · ·

silver reel (rose) wire

· · ·

secateurs (pruning shears)

· · ·

wire-cutters

· · ·

.91 florist's wires

· · ·

wreath base

· · ·

7.5 cm (3 in) wide gold ribbon

This wreath is designed to have an informal and slightly wayward look, so it is a good idea to avoid the darkest and heaviest of evergreens.

Wispy bunches of gilded seed heads set this pretty wreath apart from the normal dark green Christmas decorations. Combine them with a light mix of seasonal leaves such as ivy, mistletoe and eucalyptus, or whatever is available. The artificial roses mean that the wreath can be placed outside on a front door or, alternatively, it would look very attractive indoors. Place it where the gilding and the gold ribbons will catch the light.

1 Cover the work surface with newspaper and spread out the wheat and linseed (flax) seed heads, the artificial roses and any evergreens to be sprayed with gold paint. Here a few ivy and eucalyptus stems are spatter-sprayed, but the leaves are not covered completely. Spray the materials on one side, then turn over and spray on the other. Leave to dry.

2 Gather the wheat into bunches of four or five stalks and bind the stalks with silver reel (rose) wire. Bind the linseed (flax) into bunches of uneven lengths. Cut the evergreens into short lengths.

3 Cut several florist's wires in half and bend to make U-shaped pins. Place a bunch of evergreens over the wreath base, loop a wire pin over the stalks and press the wire ends into the base.

4 Take a bunch of wheat and a piece of mistletoe, so that the wheat seed heads cover the mistletoe stem. Pin to the base. Continue adding evergreens and the other materials all round the ring, the heads of each bunch covering the stalks of the previous one.

5 Position the sprayed artificial flowers around the ring in an asymmetrical way. Push their wire stems horizontally through the evergreens into the wreath base. Tie two ribbon bows and neaten the ends by cutting them at an angle. Push half a florist's wire through the loop at the back of each bow and insert it into the wreath.

Hang the wreath where it will catch flattering shafts of light to emphasize the gilding.
To give your Christmas decorations a co-ordinated look, you could compose a smaller version of the wreath for a table decoration.

AROMATIC CHRISTMAS WREATH

· · ·

MATERIALS

· · ·

*omorica cones or very small
fir cones*

· · ·

plastic bag

· · ·

*40 drops synthetic rose-scented
oil, 20 drops cedarwood,
20 drops frankincense,
20 drops myrrh*

· · ·

*plastic foam wreath base with
integral plastic tray*

· · ·

flower food

· · ·

3 candles

· · ·

.91 florist's wires

· · ·

artificial red berries

· · ·

secateurs (pruning shears)

· · ·

holly sprigs

· · ·

pointed stick or skewer

· · ·

large-headed red roses

*Pure rose essential oil is very
expensive, but a rose-scented
synthetic oil is acceptable here.*

Tiny fir cones tossed in rose-scented oil, cedarwood, frankincense and myrrh give this beautiful wreath a rich floral and spicy aroma that will fill the room. If possible, prepare the fir cones two or three days ahead so that they have time to absorb the scented oils. Holly with berries is often not available, so it is acceptable to use a few artificial berries instead. Remove the roses at night, if you wish, and place them in water with a little flower food.

1 Put the fir cones in a plastic bag. Mix the oils, add them to the bag and shake well for a few minutes.

2 Soak the foam wreath thoroughly in water with flower food added. Position the candles at regular intervals, pressing them down to the base of the foam.

3 Thread the end of a florist's wire around the base of each scented fir cone, pulling it firmly so that the wire is hardly visible.

4 Wire the red berries together in small bunches, leaving the wire ends long enough to press into the foam.

5 Cut off small holly twigs. Make a hole in the foam with the pointed stick or skewer and push the holly in gently. Cover the top, inner and outer sides of the foam.

6 Add the wired artificial berries towards the centre of a group of leaves to make them look authentic.

7 Cut the rose stems to about 7.5 cm (3 in), to allow the heads to sit above the holly and give them space for the petals to open. Make a hole before inserting each rose.

8 Add the fir cones, positioning them carefully to create an attractive display.

BAY AND ORANGE MANTELPIECE SWAG

· · ·

MATERIALS

· · ·

2 blocks plastic foam

· · ·

plastic cases

· · ·

knife

· · ·

secateurs (pruning shears)

· · ·

about 200 bay leaves for each 30 cm (12 in)

· · ·

silver reel (rose) wire

· · ·

dried orange slices

· · ·

wire-edged ribbon, about twice as long as the mantelpiece

Wire up the orange slices in pairs, to give extra colour impact.

Dark orange slices nestling among green bay leaves look very attractive at Christmas. Plastic cases, available from florists, link together to make up the length you need. Alternatively, you can place the plastic foam in a rectangle of chicken wire and roll it up to make a sausage shape. If you leave the bay leaves to dry out, you can use them later in the kitchen.

1 Soak the foam blocks thoroughly in water. Cut them to fit inside the plastic cases. Trim sprigs of bay leaves off the branches and push them into the foam until it is completely covered.

2 Cut 20 cm (8 in) lengths of wire. Wire the orange slices in pairs, twisting the ends together.

3 Push the wired oranges into the swag. Wind the ribbon around the whole length.

TULIP AND HOLLY WREATH

· · ·

MATERIALS

· · ·

*plastic foam ring,
25 cm (10 in) diameter*

· · ·

100 stems white tulips

· · ·

scissors

· · ·

holly with berries

*The tulip stems are pushed
fully into the foam in tight
masses, so that only their heads
are visible.*

The extravagant use of white tulips achieves a sophisticated purity in this Christmas decoration. A cushion of white blooms interspersed with glossy dark green leaves and vibrant red berries produces a wreath that can be used either on a door or, with candles, as a table centrepiece.

1 Soak the plastic foam ring in water. Cut the tulips to a stem length of approximately 3 cm (1⅛ in). Starting at the centre, work outwards in concentric circles to cover the whole surface of the plastic foam with the tulip heads.

2 Cover any exposed foam and the outside of the ring with holly leaves by pushing their stems into the foam and overlapping them flat against the edge of the ring. (You may wish to secure the leaves with .71 wire.)

3 Cut 12 stems of berries approximately 4 cm (1½ in) long and push them into the foam in two concentric circles around the ring, one towards the inside and the other towards the outside. Make sure no foam is still visible.

MISTLETOE KISSING RING
. . .

Instead of just tying a bunch of mistletoe to some strategically placed light-fitting in the hall, be creative and make a traditional kissing ring. This can be hung up as a Christmas decoration and still serve as a focal point for a seasonal kiss!

MATERIALS
. . .
scissors
. . .
7 berries-only stems of winterberry
. . .
large bunch mistletoe
. . .
twine
. . .
1 twisted cane ring
. . .
1 roll tartan (plaid) ribbon

Very simple in its construction; this design does require a reasonable quantity of good quality, fresh mistletoe for it to survive the full festive season.

1 Cut the stems of the winterberry into 18 cm (7 in) lengths. Divide the mistletoe into 14 substantial stems and make the smaller sprigs into bunches by tying with twine. Attach a branch of winterberry on to the outside of the ring with the twine. Add a stem, or bunch, of mistletoe so that it overlaps about one-third of the length of winterberry, and bind in place. Bind on another stem of winterberry, overlapping the mistletoe.

2 Repeat the sequence until the outside of the cane ring is covered in a "herringbone" pattern of materials. Cut four lengths of ribbon of approximately 60 cm (24 in) each. Tie one end of each of the pieces of ribbon to the decorated ring at four equidistant points around its circumference. Bring the four ends of the ribbon up above the ring and tie into a bow; this will enable you to suspend the finished kissing ring.

EVERGREEN TABLE SWAG

. . .

MATERIALS

. . .

knife

. . .

rope

. . .

secateurs (pruning shears)

. . .

fresh blue pine (spruce)

. . .

silver reel (rose) wire

. . .

fir cones

. . .

.91 wires

. . .

dried red chillies

. . .

glue gun and glue sticks

. . .

dried fungi

. . .

dried pomegranates

. . .

reindeer moss

. . .

dried lavender

. . .

dried red roses

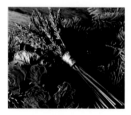

Decorate the blue pine (spruce) swag with crossed bunches of red roses and lavender.

This seasonal table decoration is made in two halves so it is easier to handle. Conceal the join with large dried materials such as extra pomegranates and fir cones. Use the blue pine (spruce) fresh; it will dry out naturally without losing its colour or needles, and has a wonderful scent. Take great care when using the hot glue gun; any glue that gets on to the display by accident can be covered with the addition of a little moss. If you want to place your swag above an open fire, make sure it is well away from the heat.

1 Cut two lengths of rope; their combined length should be the length you want the swag to be. Cut the blue pine (spruce) stems to about 20 cm (8 in) long. Using silver reel (rose) wire, bind the stems to the rope.

2 If some of the cones are still attached to the stems, bind them to the rope with wire as well.

3 Continue the process until the whole length of both ropes has been well covered. Do not leave any gaps along the edges. Centre-wire the chillies, and fix them along the length of the swag.

4 Using a glue gun, glue the fungi, extra fir cones and pomegranates in place, at well-balanced intervals and to create an attractive design. Then add the reindeer moss to fill any spaces and to create extra colour and interest.

5 Centre-wire the lavender and roses. Fix them in groups, crossing a bunch of roses with a bunch of lavender. Twist the wire ends under the swag and tuck the sharp ends back into the bottom. You can decorate the point where the ends of the swag meet, if you like, by placing candles in terracotta pots in the centre of the display.

This festive swag will look wonderful decorating the table for a simple meal for two, or as the feature of a traditional Christmas feast.

EVERGREEN AND GOLDEN CONE SWAG

· · ·

*This simple garland is
composed of blue pine (spruce).
Other materials could include
Norwegian pine or cypress.*

This traditional Christmas decoration of blue pine (spruce), decorated with fir cones and gilded wheat, is very impressive. The hay-covered rope base is very pliable so you can drape the swag around gentle curves or allow it to hang naturally. Using a glue gun with hot glue means that the fir cones are firmly attached. Work with separate lengths of rope or one continuous length, as required to fit the space.

1 Measure the area where the swag is to hang, allowing for gentle curves and drapes, and cut the rope to the required length. Tie the twine to one end of the rope. Take handfuls of hay, wrap it around the rope and bind it with the twine. Continue adding hay until the rope is completely concealed.

2 Cut the blue pine (spruce) in short lengths. Place the first one over the hay-covered rope and bind it in place with the twine. Bind on more sprays, each one covering the stem end of the one before.

3 Gather the wheat in bunches of about six or seven heads and cut the stems to a total length of about 18 cm (7 in). Bind the stems with green twine. Place the bunches of wheat well apart on newspaper and spray the heads with gold paint. Turn them over and spray them on the other side. Leave the paint to dry. Bind bunches of gilded wheat along the swag, first on one side and then the other.

4 When the length of the swag is completed, attach the fir cones. Drizzle spots of glue on to the blue pine at intervals and press on a cone. Alternate small, rounded cones with long ones. Tie the ribbon in a bow, neaten the ends by cutting them at an angle, then thread a florist's wire through the loop at the back. Attach the bow to the centre of the swag. Hang the swag in position and adjust it so that the evergreens face outwards.

SPRUCE AND
AMARYLLIS SWAG
· · ·

MATERIALS
· · ·
3 plastic foam blocks
· · ·
knife
· · ·
*25 cm (10 in) wide strip of
chicken wire to fit mantelshelf*
· · ·
5 small metal buckets
· · ·
secateurs (pruning shears)
· · ·
2 branches blue pine (spruce)
· · ·
glass nuggets or small pebbles
· · ·
3 large green pillar candles
· · ·
4 thin green pillar candles
· · ·
fine raffia or twine
· · ·
6 stems amaryllis
· · ·
*10 sprays lichen-covered
larch twigs*
· · ·
2 large bunches purple grapes

This lavish Christmas ornament combines a rich variety of textures and colours, some traditional and some modern. Miniature buckets, available from gift shops and florists, hold candles and cut amaryllis flowers, whose smooth surfaces contrast beautifully with the textured background of blue pine (spruce). Bunches of purple grapes complete the sumptuous effect.

1 Soak the florist's foam, cut each block in half lengthways and leave to drain. Arrange the cut blocks along the chicken wire. Wrap the chicken wire around the blocks, leaving gaps for the metal buckets. Cut the blue pine (spruce) into manageable lengths and insert in the foam.

2 Place a large handful of glass nuggets or small pebbles in the bottom of each bucket, then place a large candle in three of the buckets. Tie the thin candles in pairs, using raffia or twine, and set a pair in the remaining two buckets. Add water. Add two stems of amaryllis to each large candle.

*Metal buckets hold candles
and flowers, while adding to
the silvery, frosty look.*

3 Place the buckets in or on the swag. Place larch twigs amongst the blue pine (spruce). Split up the bunches of grapes and group some in front of each bucket.

SUPPLIERS

· · ·

Most of the materials needed in this book can be obtained from Terence Moore Designs, which also undertakes special commissions and runs one-day workshops for individuals and groups. There are many stockists of floral materials, and since dried materials are more difficult to find, the following suppliers are particularly recommended. When buying dried stock, make sure that it is as fresh as possible and has plenty of colour. If the material looks muddy or is brittle to touch, then it has been in stock for a long time and should be avoided. Suppliers with only a small range of dried materials will probably have a slow turnover, so avoid buying from them.

UNITED KINGDOM

Terence Moore Designs
The Barn Workshop
Burleigh Lane, Crawley Down
West Sussex RH10 4LF
Tel/Fax: (01342) 717944.

The Bay Tree Florist
19 Upper High Street, Thame
Oxon OX9 3EX
Tel: (01844) 217993.

Bright Ideas
38 High Street, Lewes
East Sussex BN7 2LU
Tel: (01273) 474395.

Country Style
358 Fulwood Road, Ranmoor
Sheffield S10 3GD
Tel: (01742) 309067.

De La Mares Florist
Rue A Don, Grouville
Jersey, Channel Islands
Tel: (01534) 851538.

Forsyths
7 Market Place, St Albans
Herts AL3 5DK
Tel: (01727) 839702.

Hilliers Garden Centre
London Road, Windlesham
Surrey GU20 6LN
Tel: (01344) 23166.

Hilliers Garden Centre
Woodhouse Lane, Botley
Southampton S03 2EZ
Tel: (01489) 782306.

Lesley Hart Dried Flowers
37 Smith Street
Warwick CV34 4JA
Tel: (01926) 490356.

Mews Gallery
Old Stone House
23 Killenchy Comber
Co. Down
Northern Ireland
BT23 5AP
Tel: (01247) 874044.

Page and Bolland
Denscombe Mill, Shillingford
Tiverton, Devon EX16 9BH
Tel: (01398) 6283.

Three French Hens
Home Farm, Swinfern
Nr Lichfield, Staffs WS14 9QR
Tel: (01543) 481613.

UNITED STATES

American Oaks Preserving
  Company, Inc.
601 Mulberry Street
North Judson, Indiana
46366
Tel: (800) 348–5008.

Fischer & Page, Ltd.
134 West 28th Street
New York, New York
10001
Tel: (212) 645–4106.

Herb Gathering
5742 Kenwood
Kansas City, Missouri
64110
Tel: (816) 523–2653.

J&T Imports
P.O. Box 642
Solana Beach, California
92075 (wholesale).

Lee Wards
Main Office
Elgin, Illinois
60120.

Meadow Everlasting
RR 1, 149 Shabbona Road
Malta, Illinois
60150
Tel: (815) 825–2539.

Patchogue Florals Fantasyland
10 Robinson Avenue
East Patchogue, New York
11772
Tel: (516) 475–2059.

Tom Thumb Workshop
Rt. 13, Box 357
Mappsville, Virginia
23407
Tel: (757) 824–3507.

Wayside Gardens
1 Garden Lane
Hodges, South Carolina
29695–0001
Tel: (800) 845–1124.

Well-sweep Herb Farm
317 Mount Bethel Road
Port Murray, New Jersey
07865
Tel: (908) 852–5390.

CANADA

Crafts Canada
440–28 Street, NE
Calgary
Alberta
T2A 6T3
Tel: (403) 569 2355.

Multi-crafts and Gifts
2210 Thurston Drive
Ottawa
Ontario
K1G 5L5.

INDEX

· · ·

A

Achillea
  A. filipendulina (Golden
    yarrow), 14, 156
  A. ptarmica, 14, 88, 166
Adhesive, florist's, 18
Adiantum, 136
Advent candle ring, 228–9
Alchemilla mollis (Lady's
  Mantle), 14
Alstroemeria, 13
Amaranthus (Love-lies-
  bleeding), 14, 88, 95, 106,
  230
Amaryllis (*Hippeastrum*), 13
  spruce and amaryllis
    swag, 250
Ambrosina, 14
Anaphalis margaritacea (Pearl
  everlasting), 14
Anemone, 140
Apples, dried, 90, 136, 214
Aromatic Christmas wreath,
  240–1
Aromatic wreath, dried, 43
Artemisia, 60
Artichokes *see* Globe artichoke
Asparagus asparagoides
  (Smilax), 218

B

Baby gift, dried flower
  horsehoe, 222–3
Banksia serrata (Holly Oak), 15, 106
Barley garland, wild, 66
Baskets
  fruit and fungi basket rim
    decoration, 136
  hydrangea basket edging, 134
  making a border with a rope
    swag, 25
Bay leaves, 30, 78, 90, 92, 160
  bay and orange mantelpiece
    swag, 242
Beech leaves, 72
  beech leaf and dried rose
    heart, 184–5
Beetroot, 30
Berries, 178
  berried candle decoration, 143
  see also Blackberries
Birch (*Betula*), 234
Blackberries, 143
Blue pine (spruce), 104, 106, 234,
  246
  pine Christmas garland, 230–1
  spruce and amaryllis
    swag, 250
  spruce and cone wreath, 232
Boiling water treatment for cut
  flowers, 12

Bows, making fabric, 25
Branches *see* Twigs
Bridesmaid's circlet, 205, 212
Bupleurum, 100
  B. griffithii, 14

C

Cabbage candle ring, 146
Campion (*Silene pendula*), 17
Candle arrangements
  Advent candle ring, 228–9
  aromatic Christmas
    wreath, 240–1
  berried candle decoration, 143
  cabbage candle ring, 146
  candle cuff, 152
  dried rose candle rings, 151
  eucalyptus and hellebore candle
    ring, 140
  floating candle ring, 148–9
  floral chandelier, 166–7
  fresh rose candle ring, 144
  hop flower candle ring, 160
  hydrangea candle ring, 156–7
  lavender candlestick
    circlets, 150
  parrot tulip candle
    decoration, 142
  rose-perfumed candle
    pots, 154
  spruce and amaryllis
    swag, 250
  winter chandelier, 168–9
  woodland candle ring, 158–9
Candle holders, 18
Candles, wiring, 25
Canes, 18
Cape gooseberries, 228
Cape honey flower (*Protea
  compacta*), 16
Carnations, 13, 148
Carrots, 50
Carthamus, 14, 68

Celebration table decoration, 220–1
Centaurea montana
  (Knapweed), 100
Chamomile, 10
  Chamomile ring, 128
Chandeliers
  floral, 166–7
  winter, 168–9
Cherry blossom, 174
Chestnuts, 220, 230
Chicken wire, 18
  covering a frame with a
    chicken wire swag, 24
  making a swag, 24
Chillies, 74, 104, 106, 116, 148,
  234, 246
Chinese lantern (*Physalis*), 15
Chives, 32
Christmas arrangements
  Advent candle ring, 228–9
  aromatic Christmas wreath, 240
  bay and orange mantelpiece
    swag, 242
  blue pine (spruce) and amaryllis
    swag, 250
  Christmas wreath with
    artichokes, 234–5
  clementine wreath, 236
  pine Christmas garland, 230–1
  spruce and cone wreath, 232
  tulip and holly wreath, 244
  Yuletide kissing wreath, 238–9
Chrysanthemums, 12
Cinnamon sticks, 76, 78, 81, 90,
  95, 190, 228, 232
  cinnamon and orange ring, 80
Circlets
  bridesmaid's circlet, 205, 212
  hydrangea circlet, 49
  lavender candlestick circlets, 150
Clementine wreath, 236
Club wreath, nigella, 200
Conditioning of cut flowers, 12–13
Cones, 15, 62, 240
  evergreen and golden cone
    swag, 248
  gold cone garland, 74–5
  spruce and cone wreath, 232
  see also Fir cones
Conference pears, 102
Conifer, 96
Consolida (Larkspur), 15, 88,
  97, 166, 216
Copper beech (*Fagus sylvatica*), 15
copper rings, 18
Corn cobs, 224
  corn-on-the-cob
    garland, 226–7
Cornus alba (Dogwood),
  Dogwood heart, 182
Country flower wreath, 38

Country-style swag, 100
Cow parsley (Queen Anne's
  lace), 34
Cranberry heart, 176
Craspedia globosa, 196
Crescent moon wreath, 196–7
Curry flowers, 98
Cut flowers, care of, 12–13
Cynara cardunculus (Globe
  artichoke), 15, 92
  artichoke mantelpiece
    swag, 104–5
  Christmas wreath with
    artichokes, 234–5

D

Daffodils, 10, 210
Dahlia garland, white, 58–9
Daisies, 10
  Daisy napkin ring, 138
Delphiniums, 13
Diamond wreath, lavender, 199
Dill, 100, 137, 220
Dogwood (*Cornus alba*)
  heart, 182
Double leg mounts, 20
Dried materials, 14–17
  care and maintenance, 23
  steaming, 23
  wiring, 23

E

Easter wreath, 210
Echinops (Globe thistle), 108
  E. ritro, 15
  E. sphaerocephalus, 15
Elaeagnus, 210, 220
Equipment, 18–19
Eryngium (Sea holly), 17
  E. alpinum, 17, 108
Ethylene gas, 13
Eucalyptus, 10, 15, 110, 158
  E. spiralus, 97, 108
Eucalyptus arrangements
  eucalyptus and hellebore candle
    ring, 140
  eucalyptus star, 194
  eucalyptus wreath, 36
Euphorbia (Milkweed), 12
Eustoma grandiflorum, 220
Evergreens, 238
  evergreen and golden cone
    swag, 248
  evergreen table swag, 246–7
  see also blue pine
Everlasting *see* Strawflower

F

Fabric
  fabric-decorated swag, 107
  making fabric bows, 25

Fagus sylvatica (Copper beech), 15
Feather star, willow and, 192
Fennel, 138
  fennel-decorated ring, 130–1
Fir cones, 15, 54, 81, 95, 104, 106, 158, 201, 230, 234, 246, 248
  see also Cones
Fireplace swag, winter, 106
Floating candle ring, 148–9
Floral chandelier, 166–7
Floral (mossing) pins, 18
Florist's adhesive, 18
Florist's clear lacquer, 18
Florist's scissors, 18
Florist's (stem-wrap) tape, 18, 20
Florist's wire, 18
Flower and herb table swag, 95
Flowerheads
  wiring an open, 21
  wiring a rose, 22
Flowerpot swag, 88
Flowers *see* Cut flowers; Dried materials; Fresh flowers
Foliage
  conditioning, 13
  textured foliage ring, 72
  see also Evergreens
Frames, covering with chicken wire swag, 24
Freesias, 13
French lavender (*Lavandula stoechas*), 16, 60
Fresh flowers, care of, 12–13
Fresh rose candle ring, 144
Fresh rosemary heart, 187
Frosted winter garland, 81
Fruit, wiring, 22, 23
Fruit arrangements
  fruit and flower swag, 112
  fruit and fungi basket rim decoration, 136
  herb and dried fruits wreath, 52–3
Fungi, 158, 201, 224, 230, 246
  fruit and fungi basket rim decoration, 136

G
Garland rings *see* Rings
Garlands
  corn-on-the-cob garland, 226–7
  dried grass garland, 70
  frosted winter garland, 81
  geometric garland, 201
  giant sunflower garland, 56–7
  gold cone garland, 74–5
  lavender and herb garland, 60
  old-fashioned garland, 46
  pine Christmas garland, 230–1
  romantic herb garland, 55
  rose and pot-pourri garland, 54
  Valentine's garland, 206
  white dahlia garland, 58–9
  wild barley garland, 66
Garlic, 30, 116
Geometric garland, 201
Gerbera, 13, 148
Gilded spice wreath, 76–7
Globe artichoke (*Cynara cardunculus*), 15, 92
  artichoke mantelpiece swag, 104–5
  Christmas wreath with artichokes, 234–5
Globe thistle (*Echinops*), 15, 108
  globe thistle and mussel shell ring, 73
Gloves, 18
Glue guns, 18
Gold cone garland, 74–5
Golden mushrooms, 15, 62
Golden rod (*Solidago*), 220
Golden yarrow (*Achillea filipendulina*), 14, 156
Grapes, 112, 250
Grasses
  dried grass garland, 70
  dried grass harvest swag, 120
  wild barley garland, 66
  see also Wheat
Guelder rose (*Viburnum opulus*), 12, 137

H
Hanging, Provençal herb, 116
Harvest swag, dried grass, 120
Hay ropes and collars, making, 25
Hay wreath, midsummer, 68

Hazel, 64
Headdresses
  bridesmaid's circlet, 205, 212
  dried flower garland headdress, 214
Heart shapes
  beech leaf and dried rose heart, 184–5
  cranberry heart, 176
  dogwood heart, 182
  fresh rosemary heart, 187
  heart of wheat, 188
  lavender linen heart, 186
  scented rosebud heart, 180
  underwater heart, 174
  Valentine's garland, 206
  woodland heart, 178
Helenium (Sneezeweed), 112
Helianthus (Sunflower), 17, 136, 224
  giant sunflower garland, 56–7
  lavender and sunflower swag, 98
Helichrysum (Strawflower), 17
Helebores, 10
  Eucalyptus and hellebore candle ring, 140
Herbs
  flower and herb table swag, 95
  fresh herbal wreath, 30
  herb and dried fruits wreath, 52–3
  herb mantelpiece border, 92
  herb napkin ring, 138
  herbal table decoration, 137
  lavender and herb garland, 60
  Provençal herb hanging, 116
  romantic herb garland, 55
  sweet herb wreath, 32
  see also individual herbs
Hippeastrum (Amaryllis), 13
  spruce and amaryllis swag, 250

Holly, 240
  tulip and holly wreath, 244
Holly Oak (*Banksia serrata*), 15, 106
Honesty (*Lunaria*), 72, 222
Hop flowers, Hop flower candle ring, 160
Hop vine, 72, 226
  hop mantelpiece swag, 102
  hop vine rings, 54
Horseshoe baby gift, dried flower, 222–3
Hydrangea, 10, 15, 48, 214
  hydrangea basket edging, 134
  hydrangea candle ring, 156–7
  hydrangea circlet, 49
  hydrangea ring, 132

I
Immortelle (*Xeranthemum*), 15
Ivy, 112, 178, 207, 228, 236

K
Kissing rings
  mistletoe kissing ring, 245
  Yuletide kissing wreath, 238–9
Knapweed (*Centaurea montana*), 100
Kutchi fruit, 15, 106

L
Lacquer, florist's clear, 18
Lady's Mantle (*Alchemilla mollis*), 14
Larch twigs, 74, 250
Larkspur (*Consolida*), 15, 88, 97, 166, 216
Lavandula (Lavender), 16, 32, 43, 46, 48, 52, 95, 106, 107, 138, 190, 216, 230, 246
  L. stoechas (French lavender), 16, 60
Lavandula (Lavender) arrangements
  dried lavender wreath, 44
  lavender candlestick circlets, 150
  lavender diamond wreath, 199
  lavender and herb garland, 60
  lavender linen heart, 186
  lavender and seagrass wreath, 42
  lavender and sunflower swag, 98
Leaves, 134
  wiring, 23
  see also Bay; Beech; Foliage; Oak; Virginia Creeper
Leg mounts, 20
Lemons, 112, 136
Lilac (*Syringa*), 12
  white lilac ring, 126

Limes, 112
Linseed, 120, 196, 238
Lovage, 60
Love-in-a-mist (*Nigella damascena*), 16
Love-lies-bleeding (*Amaranthus*), 14, 88, 95, 106, 230
Lunaria (Honesty), 72, 222
Lupins, 13

M
Mace, 76
Mantelpiece arrangements
artichoke mantelpiece swag, 104–5
bay and orange mantelpiece swag, 242
herb mantelpiece border, 92
hop mantelpiece swag, 102
Marigold (*Tagetes erecta*), 16, 38
Marjoram (*Origanum marjorana*), 16, 30, 43, 106, 137
Midsummer hay wreath, 68
Milkweed (*Euphorbia*), 12
Mint (*Mentha*), 16, 30, 130, 137
Mintola balls, 16
Mirror frames, covering with chicken wire swag, 24
Mistletoe kissing ring, 245
Mixed swag, 94
Mosses, 16
moss and twig wreath, 62
Mossing (floral) pins, 18
Mother's Day wreath, 208
Mushrooms, dried, 15, 62
Mussel shell ring, globe thistle and, 73

N
Napkin rings
daisy, 138
herb, 138
Nicandra (*Physalodes*), 16
Nigella, 200, 216
N. damascena (Love-in-a-mist), 16
N. orientalis, 16, 120
Nigella club wreath, 200
Night-lights, 137
Nutmegs, 76
Nuts, 81
wiring, 23

O
Oak (*Quercus*), 16, 158
Omorica cones, 240
Oranges, dried, 52, 76, 78, 90, 106, 136, 168, 228
bay and orange mantelpiece swag, 242

cinnamon and orange ring, 80
Oregano (*Origanum vulgare*), 16, 88, 95, 97, 116, 128, 216

P
Paeonia (Peony), 16, 88, 95, 97, 107, 156, 166, 214
steaming dried, 23
Pansy, 114
Papaver (Poppy), 12, 16, 52, 232
poppy spade wreath, 198
Paper ribbon, 18
Parrot tulip candle decoration, 142
Parsley, 32, 130
Pear blossom, 208
Pearl everlasting (*Anaphalis margaritacea*), 14
Pears
Conference, 102
dried, 90
Peony (*Paeonia*), 16, 88, 95, 97, 107, 156, 166, 214
steaming dried, 23
Phalaris, 120, 222
Physalis (Chinese lantern), 15
Physalodes (Nicandra), 16
Picture frames, covering with chicken wire swag, 24
Pine *see* Blue pine
Pipping technique, 21
plastic foam rings, 18
Pliers, 19
Polyanthus, 210
Pomegranates, 104, 234, 246
Poppy (*Papaver*), 12, 16, 52, 232
poppy spade wreath, 198
Pot-pourri
pot-pourri ring, 164
rose and pot-pourri garland, 54
Protea compacta (Cape honey flower), 16
Provençal herb hanging, 116
Pruning shears, 19
Psylliostachys suworowii (Rat's-tail statice), 17
Pussy willow (*Salix caprea*), 208
Pyracantha, 236

Q
Queen Anne's lace, 34
Quercus (Oak), 16, 158

R
Raffia, 19
Rat's-tail statice (*Psylliostachys suworowii*), 17
Rhododendron, 12
Ribbon
paper, 18
satin, 19

Ring arrangements
Advent candle ring, 228
cabbage candle ring, 146
chamomile ring, 128
cinnamon and orange ring, 80
daisy and herb napkin rings, 138
dried rose candle rings, 151
eucalyptus and hellebore candle ring, 140
fennel-decorated ring, 130–1
floating candle ring, 148–9
fresh rose candle ring, 144
globe thistle and mussel shell ring, 73
hop flower candle ring, 160
hydrangea candle ring, 156–7
hydrangea ring, 132
mistletoe kissing ring, 245
pot-pourri ring, 164
small fresh rose Valentine's ring, 207
textured foliage ring, 72
white lilac ring, 126
woodland candle ring, 158–9
Rings
copper or steel, 18
copper or steel preparation, 24
plastic foam, 18
Romantic herb garland, 55
Rope swags
making, 24
making a basket border with, 25
Rosa (Rose), 17, 34, 88, 95, 96, 97, 106, 107, 108, 152, 156, 166, 178, 214, 216, 220, 222, 230, 240, 246
R. paleander, 17
conditioning, 12, 13
steaming dried, 23
wiring a rose head, 22
Rose arrangements
beech leaf and dried rose heart, 184–5
dried rose candle rings, 151
dried rose wreath, 48

fresh rose candle ring, 144
rose and pot-pourri garland, 54
rose-perfumed candle pots, 154
scented rosebud heart, 180
small fresh rose Valentine's ring, 207
starfish and rose table decoration, 162
Rose (silver reel) wire, 19
Rose stripper, 19
Rosehips, 143
rosehip wreath, 40
Rosemary, 11, 30, 52, 92, 128, 137, 208
fresh rosemary heart, 187

S
Sage, 32, 50, 116
Salix caprea (Pussy willow), 208
Sanfordii, 17
Satin ribbon, 19
Scented rosebud heart, 180
Scissors, florist's, 18
Sea holly (*Eryngium*), 17, 108
Seagrass wreath, lavender and, 42
Searing method, 12
Seashore wreath, 82–3
Seaside swag, 108
Secateurs (pruning shears), 19
Senecio laxifolius, 220
Shaker-style spice wreath, 78
Shells, 82, 108, 110
globe thistle and mussel shell ring, 73
Silene pendula (Campion), 17
Silver reel (rose) wire, 19
Single leg mounts, 20
Smilax (*Asparagus asparagoides*), 218
Sneezeweed (*Helenium*), 112
Solidago (Golden rod), 220
Solidaster, 17
Spade wreath, poppy, 198
Spices
gilded spice wreath, 76–7
Shaker-style spice wreath, 78
spicy star wall decoration, 190
Spiral, wheatsheaf, 118
Spring flower swag, 114–15
Spruce, 104, 106, 234, 246
pine Christmas garland, 230–1
spruce and amaryllis swag, 250
spruce and cone wreath, 232
Star shapes
eucalyptus star, 194
spicy star wall decoration, 190
willow and feather star, 192
Starfish, 108, 162, 168
starfish and rose table decoration, 162

starfish swag, 110
Statice, 17, 148
Stay wires, making, 20
Steaming technique for dried
    flowers, 23
Stem-wrap (florist's) tape, 18, 20
Stems
    composite (units), 21
    conditioning hollow-stemmed
        flowers, 13
    extending the length, 21
    wrapping to straighten, 13
Strawflower (*Helichrysum*), 17
String, 19
Summer table swag, 97
Summer wreath, glorious, 34
Sunflower (*Helianthus*), 17, 136,
    224
    giant sunflower garland, 56–7
    lavender and sunflower swag, 98
Swag arrangements
    artichoke mantelpiece
        swag, 104–5
    bay and orange mantelpiece
        swag, 242
    country-style swag, 100
    dried grass harvest swag, 120
    evergreen and golden cone
        swag, 248
    evergreen table swag, 246–7
    fabric-decorated swag, 107
    flower and herb table swag, 95
    flowerpot swag, 88
    fruit and flower swag, 112
    hop mantelpiece swag, 102
    lavender and sunflower
        swag, 98
    mixed swag, 94
    seaside swag, 108
    spring flower swag, 114–15
    spruce and amaryllis
        swag, 250
    starfish swag, 110
    summer table swag, 97
    table swag, 218
    table-edge swag, 96
    wedding swag, 216
    winter fireplace swag, 106
Swags
    chicken wire, 24
    rope, 24, 25
Syringa (Lilac), 12
    white lilac ring, 126

T
Table decorations
    celebration table
        decoration, 220–1
    evergreen table swag, 246–7
    flower and herb table swag, 95
    herbal table decoration, 137

starfish and rose table
    decoration, 162
summer table swag, 97
table swag, 218–19
table-edge swag, 96
Tagetes erecta (Marigold), 16, 38
Tape, florist's (stem-wrap), 18, 20
Taping technique, 20
Tarragon, 60
Tea-lights, 137
Techniques
    chicken wire swags, 24
    conditioning, 12–13
    copper or steel ring
        preparation, 24
    extending stem length, 21
    fabric bows, 25
    hay ropes or collar, 25
    leg mounts, 20
    making stay wires, 20
    pipping, 21
    rope swags, 24, 25
    steaming flowers, 23
    taping, 20
    units, 21
    wiring a candle, 25
    wiring flowers, 22, 23
    wiring fruit and nuts, 23
    wiring fruit and vegetables, 22
    wiring leaves, 23
    wiring an open flowerhead, 21
    wiring a rose head, 22
Textured foliage ring, 72
Thanksgiving wreath, 224–5
Thyme, 116
Ti tree, 214
Tindori, 148
Tolbos (Top brush), 17
Triticale, 120
Tulip
    Parrot tulip candle
        decoration, 142
    tulip and holly wreath, 244
Turnips, 50
Twigs, 74, 158, 201, 230, 234,

250
    moss and twig wreath, 62
    twiggy wreath, 64
Twine, 19

U
Underwater heart, 174
Units, 21

V
Valentine's arrangements
    small fresh rose Valentine's
        ring, 207
    Valentine's garland, 206
    see also Heart shapes
Vegetables, 22
    vegetable garden wreath, 50
Viburnum opulus (Guelder
    rose), 12, 137
Viola, 114
Virginia creeper
    leaves, 143

W
Wedding arrangements
    bridesmaid's circlet, 205, 212
    dried flower garland
        headdress, 214
    wedding swag, 216
Wheat, 17, 97, 238, 248
    heart of wheat, 188
    wheatsheaf spiral, 118
White dahlia garland, 58–9
White lilac ring, 126
Wild barley garland, 66
Willow, 194
    Willow and feather
        star, 192
Window decoration, 90–1
Winter chandelier, 168–9
Winter fireplace swag, 106
Winter garland, frosted, 81
Winterberry, 245
Wire
    chicken, 18, 24

florist's, 18
    silver reel (rose), 19
Wiring techniques
    extending length of a stem, 21
    leg mounts, 20
    open flowerheads, 21
    pipping, 21
    stay wires, 20
    units, 21
    wiring a candle, 25
    wiring flowers, 22, 23
    wiring fruit and nuts, 23
    wiring fruit and vegetables, 22
    wiring leaves, 23
    wiring a rose head, 22
Woodland candle ring, 158–9
Woodland heart, 178
Wreaths
    aromatic Christmas
        wreath, 240–1
    Christmas wreath with
        artichokes, 234–5
    clementine wreath, 236
    country flower wreath, 38
    crescent moon wreath, 196–7
    dried aromatic wreath, 43
    dried lavender wreath, 44
    dried rose wreath, 48
    Easter wreath, 210
    eucalyptus wreath, 36
    fresh herbal wreath, 30
    gilded spice wreath, 76–7
    glorious summer wreath, 34
    herb and dried fruits
        wreath, 52–3
    lavender diamond wreath, 199
    lavender and seagrass wreath, 42
    midsummer hay wreath, 68
    moss and twig wreath, 62
    Mother's Day wreath, 208
    nigella club wreath, 200
    poppy spade wreath, 198
    rosehip wreath, 40
    seashore wreath, 82–3
    Shaker-style spice wreath, 78
    spruce and cone wreath, 232
    sweet herb wreath, 32
    Thanksgiving wreath, 224–5
    tulip and holly wreath, 244
    twiggy wreath, 64
    vegetable garden wreath, 50
    Yuletide kissing wreath, 238–9

X
Xeranthemum (Immortelle), 15

Y
Yuletide kissing wreath, 238–9

Z
Zinnias, 148

NOTES

NOTES

NOTES

NOTES

NOTES

NOTES

NOTES

Notes